THE NAKED CONFIDENCE
HOW TO TRANSFORM YOUR BATTLE WITH FOOD INTO SELF-L
CORTNEY CRIBARI

Cortney Cribari is a life student and servant, who shares what she has learned and experienced. Cortney is not a registered dietician or certified nutritionist. Cortney Cribari is not responsible for what happens in your life as a result of this book. The premise of author's information is your health is based on personal experience, discipline, medical history and level of commitment.

The information in this book reflects the author's personal success, experience and opinions and is not intended to replace medical advice. Before beginning this or any nutritional, diet or exercise regimen consult your physician to be sure it is appropriate for you.

Copyright © 2016 Inspiro Studio LLC

All rights reserved. This publication is copyright. No part of it may be reproduced or transmitted in any form without the written permission of the author.

Published by Inspiro Studio LLC
Designed by Cortney and Todd Cribari
Printed by CreateSpace, An Amazon.com Company

Author: Cortney Cribari
Editor: Kimberly Castleberry
Food and Lifestyle Photographer: Todd Domenic Cribari
Food Stylist: Cortney Cribari
Title: The Naked Confidence Cookbook: How To Transform Your Battle With Food InTo Self-Love and Your Best Body
ISBN: 9781535245975
Subject: Cooking, Health & Healing, Gluten-Free, Special Diets, Nutrition, Self-Help

cortneycribari.com
instagram.com/@cortneycribari
facebook.com/cortneycribari

To all my loving and dear friends who have made a difference in my life and encouraged me to be authentically me. To my husband, Todd, for being my biggest angel and guiding light. I love you with all my heart.

FOREWORD

BY DR. KEERTHY SUNDER, M.D.

The human body is a perfectly designed machine with many systems working together peacefully. When one of those systems goes down or is thrown off balance, the result is like a domino falling, with a litany of health problems likely to follow. The digestive system is especially critical in our overall health and wellness, as it and our immune system our closely linked. Research shows that 70 percent of our immune system is located in the gut as they are closely linked. So when our digestive system fails, a number of chronic problems can arise like acid reflux, indigestion and irritable bowel disease.

It is critical that we approach our gut with confidence and provide it wholesome nutrition to boost immunity and prevent the now well-known ravages of "Leaky Gut Syndrome" from nutritionally depleted foods. Further, since over 50% of individuals with eating disorders abuse drugs and/or alcohol, the co-occurrence of these disorders creates an environment for "Reward Deficiency Syndrome" in the brain, leading to a depletion of multiple neurotransmitters essential for a thriving body and high performing brain

If we are to perform at our absolute best throughout our lifetime, we need to adopt a diligent and compassionate approach to mastering our psychology and physiology. Cortney Cribari exemplifies that in her timeless book synthesized from her personal transformational experience. She is on a mission to help transform those who are struggling with food by giving them practical tools that can be applied immediately. Cortney's personal battle has led her to deeply understand the importance of taking care of the gut, the mind and the brain, and develop a self-reflective plan toward lifelong wellness.

The Naked Confidence CookBook is so much more than a cookbook. You will come away knowing how to take back control of your appetite, your cravings, your conflicts with your body image and your sense of self. She gives you practical tips on how to break free from the clutches of self-doubt and re-engineer a wholesome self. With personal examples, she teaches you how to cook your way to inner freedom, a radiant body and boundless joy with kindness and compassion.

Thank you Cortney for an extraordinary contribution. Men and women all over the world will be inspired to transform their lives one recipe at a time and one day at a time. Yours is a much-needed voice in the health and wellness community.

Keerthy Sunder, M.D., is an integrative psychiatrist and chief medical officer of the Mind & Body Treatment and Research Institute. He is the author of Face Your Addiction and Save Your Life, an international best seller. Visit his website at www.mindandbodytreatment.com.

"The Naked Confidence CookBook is so much more than a cookbook. You will come away knowing how to take back control of your appetite, your cravings, your conflicts with your body image and your sense of self."
- Dr. Keerthy Sunder, M.D.

CONTENTS

My Story — 8
Welcome Letter — 11
Part 1 - The Struggle — 13
Part 2 - The Rise — 31
Part 3 - The Triumph — 43

Healthy Cooking Preparation Steps — 47
Friendly Foods Grocery List — 50
Killer Foods That Slow Weight Loss — 52
Getting Started Eating Plan — 55
Fat Melting Eating Plan — 56

Recipes — 59
Breakfast — 61
Eggs & More — 62
Green Smoothies — 79
Protein Shakes — 85

Lunch — 95
Power Salads — 95
Soulful Soups — 111
Bunless Burgers — 115

Healthy Snacks — 119

Divine Dinners — 127
Free Range Chicken & Turkey — 128
Fish — 137
Grass-Fed Beef — 141
Grill-It-Up — 143
Satisfying Sides — 153

Guilt-Free Desserts — 161

Naked Confidence Lifestyle Rituals — 172

Recipe Index — 178

MY STORY

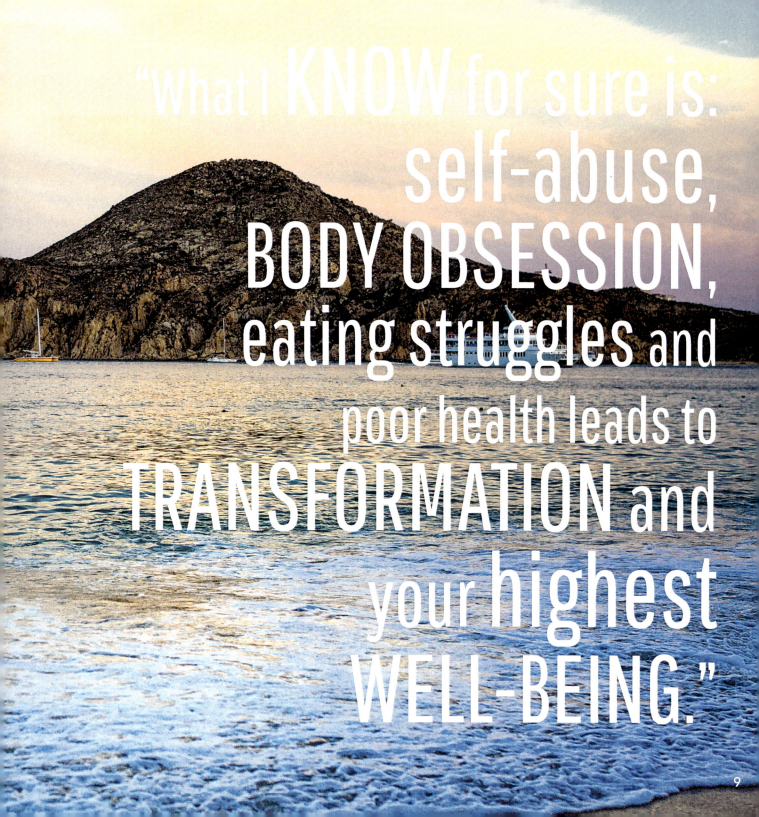

"What I KNOW for sure is: self-abuse, BODY OBSESSION, eating struggles and poor health leads to TRANSFORMATION and your highest WELL-BEING."

Welcome to Naked Confidence

Dear Friend,

I am honored to share my life-changing health evolution with you. Naked Confidence is all about loving yourself more so you can be confident, healthy and happy with who you are; and tapping into the strength that is already inside of you.

I wrote *The Naked Confidence Cookbook* as if I were talking to my best friend. I hope I I find that in you. You and I are not much different. We are both going through life doing the best we can: learning, growing and sometimes making mistakes along the way.

Perhaps you too have felt that deep down inside you deserve nothing less than an amazing life. This book is an invitation into a brand new reality full of self-love and total health. I believe life is a spiritual journey, every struggle is a learning opportunity for deeper self-exploration and personal growth. As I share everything I know, may my truths offer you comfort and something deeper than the ups and downs of daily life.

After taking years to reflect on my health crisis turned mission to heal my body; after spending thousands of dollars working with western medicine MDs, nutritionists, naturopathic doctors and practitioners; and after becoming a certified yoga and fitness instructor, as well as an expert on healthy living, I'm on the other side. You know as well as I do that there is a ton of information out there about health and food. You also know that so much of that information can be confusing, overwhelming and misleading. I've waded through it all. And what I can offer you now is a guided tour to your highest well-being--without bias, empty promises or false ideas.

Maybe my words will give you permission to release any pain and mistakes of the past, start fresh and become stronger than you've ever been. *The Naked Confidence Cookbook* is not your average cookbook. Going beyond healthy recipes, I reveal some of my darkest moments, which until now, I've only shared with my closest friends. *What most people don't know about me is I used to torture myself to be thin.*

In my teens and for most of my adult life I struggled with unhealthy eating habits, drugs, toxic relationships, body image issues and insecurities that manifested into self-abuse, Irritable Bowel Syndrome (IBS), candida overgrowth and Hashimoto's Thyroiditis disease.

My health struggles felt like a never-ending battle that was waging war against my soul. When you have physically and emotionally suffered for as long as I had, you have two choices: keep getting sicker and living miserably, or do everything you can to feel better and enjoy life. I chose the latter.

Today, I truly honor my body and love the skin I'm in. I am so grateful for happiness that has come from my decision to seek the truth and make health my #1 priority in life.

"Without health, life is not life; it is only a state of languor and suffering." -- Francois Rabelais, a major French Renaissance writer, doctor and humanist

My truth: total body success is a reality once you have tortured yourself long enough. I believe miracles come from struggle.

Over the last three years, I have collected my 100 favorite recipes as a personal passion to stay the course on my journey, meet body goals and help my husband and clients to be as healthy as possible. Along the way I have cracked the code to effortless weight loss by discovering how to make the process as pain-free and enjoyable as possible.

The quest: to regain control over your individual health SO YOU CAN HAVE incredible body confidence, super-charged energy and be ridiculously happy with yourself. I swear by every single recipe and lesson in this book as they have healed my body and soul.

Like I said earlier, this isn't a garden variety cookbook. With those recipes comes my story and the life lessons I have learned along the way. And as a special bonus, I've included my Naked Confidence Eating Plans where I take all of the work out of it for you. Follow these and you'll never have to think about when and what to eat again.

I have no doubt that once you dive into this book, you will be inspired to find yourself again--just like I did. Weight loss will no longer be a never-ending battle. Food will no longer be your worst enemy. You now have an easy tool for learning to eat the right foods and take care of yourself.

WE all deserve a healthy, stress-free and beautiful life. Your highest well-being and true beauty is reflected in how often health and self-love influence your decisions. Together let's be shining lights to the world.

Xo, Cort

THE STRUGGLE
PART 1

"Your personal story distinguishes you and sets you apart from every other human being on the planet."
- Bo Eason, ex NFL player and public speaker

Honor Your Body - Realizing There's a Problem

Have you ever made yourself sick from overeating?

If you struggle with eating and food, I know how you feel. We are not alone. According to the National Eating Disorder Association (nationaleatingdisorders.org) in the United States, 20 million women and 10 million men suffer from a significant eating disorder at some time in their life, including anorexia nervosa, bulimia nervosa, binge eating disorder, or other specified feeding or eating disorders (Wade, Keski-Rahkonen, & Hudson, 2011). Let that stat sink in: many people don't eat in a healthy way.

An eating disorder is defined as: any of a range of psychological disorders characterized by abnormal or disturbed eating habits.

Eating disorders are often not obvious, not typically reported and hidden by shame and guilt. Plus, in our culture we are bombarded with unhealthy messages around food and body image, so much so that it perpetuates much of our body dissatisfaction and disordered eating attitudes and behaviors. Millions of us are suffering from a disorder that is physically, emotionally and spiritually destructive.

What's worse is that it starts early. By age 6, girls start to express concerns about their own weight or body shape. Forty to sixty percent of elementary school girls (ages 6-12) are concerned about their weight or about becoming too fat. This concern can endure through life (Smolak, 2011).

I was 16 years old when I knew I had a problem with binge eating. It was my birthday and my high school sweetheart, Adam, took me out to dinner at Jakers, the local steakhouse in my hometown of Great Falls, Montana. It was one of my favorite places to go -- and, yes, I still love steak!

I gorged that night. When it came to ordering dessert there was no holding back. It was my birthday! So I ordered Jaker's signature Mudd Pie. This was no ordinary pie. It completely filled a normal size dinner plate and was about 4 inches high of ice cream, cookie crust, hot fudge and whip cream.

Adam only took a couple bites so basically I ate the whole thing by myself. I was 108 pounds at the time. When we got back to my house, I ran straight to the bathroom sick to my stomach. I sat on the toilet for an hour that night contemplating how I was going to rid my body of all the food I stuffed down my mouth so I could feel better. It was the longest hour ever, sick with stomach cramps and nausea with no relief. There was nothing I could do but wait it out.

My mom and Adam were outside the door checking in on me but there was nothing they could do. I just wanted to be left alone in my misery. I felt so embarrassed. I had totally ruined the special birthday date Adam had planned for me. That night was the first time I had ever thought about making myself throw up or go to the bathroom after binge eating. This was the start of my obsession.

Whether you wish to say these words out loud or read them silently to yourself, if you can relate, please repeat the following healing mantra:

> Even when I am embarrassed by my actions, I deserve more love, not less. I am open to receiving all the health, support, love and kindness I deserve.

Lesson #1: Eating to make yourself sick is a form of self-abuse. You must learn to eat with care and mindfulness.

"That night was the first time I had ever thought about making myself throw up or go to the bathroom after binge eating. This was the start of my obession."

Be Honest With Yourself - Facing a Problem

When body frustration takes over what measures are you willing to take to be skinny?

According to eatingdisorderhope.com, 50% of teenage girls and 30% of teenage boys use unhealthy weight control behaviors such as smoking cigarettes, vomiting, and taking laxatives to control their weight.

Throughout high school, I continued with my binge eating episodes and had found an answer to my problem. Laxatives became my best friend. So much so that if I didn't have enough money to buy a box then I would steal them from the neighborhood grocery story.

At the time I didn't think I was doing anything wrong. Rather I thought I was a rebel. The reality was I had become a laxative abuser. Even though I was raised in a great family and, of course, knew stealing was wrong, somehow I was able to justify my behavior as a necessity. So, I would fill my purse with boxes of poop pills and just walk out of the grocery store.

Thank God I never got caught. I was too embarrassed to ask my mom for money to buy laxatives. The bigger truth is I was hiding my habit from her so she wouldn't know I had a problem. It became my own destructive secret.

The quest for body perfection can be damaging. There is constant communication of expectations that tell us being imperfect is synonymous with being unattractive. Everywhere we turn, there are messages that reinforce the false idea of health, beauty and the mold we are supposed to fit. So, we hide our real struggles and protect ourselves from shame, judgment and criticism by seeking safety in pretending to be perfect and that everything is okay.

If you have struggled with a similar issue, offer your heart the support it needs to come out of hiding by repeating this healing mantra:

> Whenever I'm ashamed or feeling guilty, I deserve more love, not less. On my worst day, I deserve more love, not less. I am precious. It's my job to protect my body. I will allow no harm to myself because I love myself.

Lesson #2: A quick fix never eliminates the problem. Be courageous and face the root of the issue.

Protect Yourself - Leaving a Toxic Relationship

Have you ever noticed that those closest to you can harm your well-being the most?

I graduated high school in 2000 and was off to the University of Montana for college. It was such an exciting time. I was no longer dating Adam and exploring my newfound freedom. My laxative problem had come to a temporary stop because I had found something much more effective and exciting.

I was going into my sophomore year when I met my first serious college boyfriend. Little did I know that the next year would turn into the darkest time of my life.

I was a normal college girl who would party and go out with girlfriends on the weekends but there was never heavy drugs involved. He took partying to a whole other level than I had ever experienced before. It was New Year's Eve of 2001 when I first learned he was doing cocaine. Cocaine use is a growing issue on college campuses, with national reports showing an increase in use among students and young adults. An estimated 5% of college students use cocaine during their time in school.

According to addictionhope.com, research shows that almost 70% percent of cocaine users began the drug after entering college. These findings are significant and warrant greater attention about the use of this illicit drug on college campuses. The effects of cocaine often appeal to students who are looking for increased stimulation to study, party, or keep up with the demands of an overloaded schedule.

Of course any good girl's natural reaction would be, "Oh my God, I can't believe you do cocaine!" However, my deep desire to be loved accepted dating a man who was a drug user and I created an environment that eventually caused me to try it.

The first time I ever tried cocaine, I was in his small studio apartment. He brought out the cocaine and divided the powdery substance into 2-inch thin lines, one for me and one for him, with his credit card. He rolled up a dollar bill, used it like a straw and snorted one of the lines up his nose. Then he gave me the rolled up dollar bill for me to use.

I instantly felt a rush like a shot of adrenaline directly into my veins throughout my whole body. His favorite drink of choice to accompany the drug was champagne. He prefered Moet. So we popped a bottle, poured ourselves a glass and continued to snort 2 to 3 more lines each.

All of a sudden, I felt like I was in a rap video with the hip-hop music blaring from the speakers.

At this point I was totally high and I instantly fell in love with it. I know now how people can get so easily hooked after one time. It's not the type of drug where you are out of it. You have complete bodily function with hyper focus and energy. My personality became inflamed. I felt like a million bucks, unstoppable and a total rockstar.

My laxative problem became non-existent because I had found cocaine. Cocaine is the perfect diuretic and gave me the best of both worlds; the drug supressed my appetite for hours and also stimulated my bowels. So I spent the next year of my life as a cokehead, thanks to my dangerous attraction to bad boys.

Here I was 20 years old, partying like a rockstar with my bad boy boyfriend in the little college town of Missoula, Montana. Cocaine, champagne and hip-hop music became our weekend pre-party ritual at his studio then we would meet up with our group of friends at the local dance club called The Boardroom.

We would dance the night away, come home to his studio and continue to do more drugs. We were the life of the party. I thought it was true love. I got carried away by false love and decided to move in with him. That decision ended up becoming one of the worst mistakes of my life. We found a 2-bedroom apartment and very quickly our place became a nonstop party house.

My habit quickly turned from a weekend party ritual to a new normal, where doing a line of cocaine before homework or vacuuming became a way of life. In hindsight, I was on the edge of becoming an addict, with an available mound stashed above our kitchen cabinets for my personal use at all times.

I used to think my lifestyle was normal, that using cocaine was no big deal. I wasn't in my right mind. I was living in my ego of neediness. At the time, I was down to one meal per day as the cocaine killed my appetite and any food I did eat, the drug made me poop out. I was as skinny as I had ever been: 5'8" and 105-pounds.

As you can imagine, things started to get ugly. There was a price to pay for this addict lifestyle and my world quickly turned dark. Physically, I had lost my menstrual period because of malnutrition and the toll of partying. Whenever my boyfriend wasn't high he was very difficult to get along with so we fought nonstop. Our house was a battle zone with emotional abuse running rampant. I felt horrible that I chose to be with a man who didn't care about my well-being so why did I love him?

During fights there was violence: holes punched in walls next to my head, uncontrollable aggression, etc...I thought it was a matter of time before there would be physical abuse. My personal items started disappearing, like the Mac laptop I used for school. Remember the colored Mac laptops? Mine had gone missing. My guess, it was pawned for drugs. The late nights made it impossible for me to make my early morning classes and my professors started noticing my absence. They warned me to get it together or they would fail me. My mom could sense what was going on and how miserable I had become. She kept telling me to leave over and over but it took me having to be pushed to the edge to listen.

It was 6 a.m., the sun was starting to rise and I was wide awake on a bender. I had taken too much, shivering with cold sweats and unable to fall asleep. He was still not home from partying and at that time I suspected cheating. I was officially living a nightmare. In that moment, I realized the way I was living was not who I was raised to be and I had to get myself out. He was on a downward spiral and I felt him taking me down too. The fighter in me woke up.

The next night when he came home, we got into another fight over nothing. I said, "That's it, I'm done and leaving you." I left. The next day I returned (with my good friend Pat for protection), got my stuff and never looked back.

Years later I ran into a mutual friend of ours. She told me my ex went to rehab twice and finally got clean from drugs and alcohol. He now works in a rehab facility helping others get sober. I hated him for a long time but with forgiveness comes healing. The truth is I participated in toxic behavior and accepted an abusive relationship because I didn't love myself. I take full responsibility for allowing toxic people into my life. I wish him well and send him love.

To help the sometimes overwhelming challenges of life into graceful moments of healing, please repeat the following mantra with me if there is anything in your past that is still hurting you:

> Now matter the past that I've survived, I deserve more love, not less. Even when life seems like it can't get any worse, I deserve more love, not less. I love the part of me who so desperately wants to be loved even when others treat me poorly. No one can hurt me because I choose to love myself more than anyone else does. I am unbreakable.

Lesson #3: Who you allow close to you affects your health and well-being. People who love you care about your well-being and do not cause you harm. If you are in an unhealthy relationship that causes you pain and suffering, get out as fast as you can because you deserve nothing but love in this world.

Relationships - Setting Healthy Boundaries Exercise

Let's build you the RIGHT support system and healthy environment. One of the biggest secrets to success is to only surround yourself with the people who believe in you, support your healthy choices and step away from the ones who don't!

Step 1: Write a list of the top 20 friends, family, coworkers and people you know.

1. _____
2. _____
3. _____
4. _____
5. _____
6. _____
7. _____
8. _____
9. _____
10. _____
11. _____
12. _____
13. _____
14. _____
15. _____
16. _____
17. _____
18. _____
19. _____
20. _____

Step 2: Who on the list above is contaminating and who is contributing?

Contaminating	Contributing

Get Educated About What You Eat - Stopping Diet Pills

Do you keep having the same struggles over and over and feel like you never have things figured out when it comes to weight loss?

In 2004 I graduated college with a double major in Political Science and Communication Studies from the University of Montana. During this time I met my ex-husband. He was tall, dark, handsome and graduating from law school. He promised me the world and to make all my dreams come true. I thought he was my life's answer and for a needy 22-year-old girl, he was my knight in shining armor.

He proposed and we were married on August 6th, 2006. Six months before our wedding I was 20 pounds overweight, done with drugs and off laxatives. However, I was still binge eating and it finally caught up to my waistline. At that time, I had no idea how to eat healthy or lose weight in a mindful way. And like any girl getting married, I wanted to be in the best shape of my life for my wedding.

I went into major wedding slimdown mode. This time I decided to go without laxatives because I knew the discomfort so I chose diet pills. I purchased a popular appetite-suppressant diet pill that would trick my brain into thinking I had just eaten a large meal. It became my go-to daily habit for the next 6 months. According to the Lighthouse Recovery Institute, each year the diet pill industry is estimated to produce between $20-$40 billion in revenue. At any given time, there are over 100 million dieters in the US.

I took 2 pills, 3 times a day at breakfast, lunch and dinner. It completely shut off my appetite and forced my body into starvation mode. When I was hungry, I would eat cereal and SlimFast shakes for 4 months straight. By the time my wedding came, I had hit my weight loss goal and got back into a size 3 but I basically starved myself to get there.

After the wedding I went off the diet pills and was fatigued, had wrecked my metabolism and gained backed most of the weight within 30 days. It was the beginning of my autoimmune issues. Whatever arises in your life, reveals the next moment of healing in your health evolution, please repeat the following mantra:

> I do the best I can. I always have an opportunity to be healthy. I am so grateful to receive the support I need to help me overcome any struggle. I am thankful.

Lesson #4: You can increase your will power and have greater hunger control without diet pills by eating the right foods and creating a healthy environment. Take the time to get educated and learn what foods give you maximum metabolic benefits that help you lose weight naturally and clean up your environment.

Maximize Hunger Control - Increasing Will Power

We all know that a lack of will power is a problem. Research shows that Americans believe a lack of will power is the biggest barrier to adopting a healthier lifestyle and that will power is something they can learn or improve – if only they had more money, energy or confidence in their ability to change. The truth is will power is not an inner strength or emotional issue but a metabolic and environmental problem. The key is structuring your environment to increase the likelihood of making healthy choices at any given time.

The good news is...taking crazy diet pills to reduce your appetite -- which can increase your risk of heart attack and stroke -- does not have to be your future. I have found two critical steps to increase your discipline with food and stop bad eating patterns. My two steps will help you eat without stressing about food and lose weight at the same time. As a healthy lifestyle expert, I have identified four different stages of the health evolution:

Sick and/or Overweight:
Plagued with health conditions, always tired and hungry, nutritionally deficient, depressed, a BMI (Body Mass Index) of 30 or greater, or an avid junk food eater with a large amount of weight to lose from 30 to 100-plus pounds.

Unhappy and Unsatisfied with Your Body:
Plagued with body shaming issues and insecurities, never satisfied with appearance and has a difficult time getting results, low self-esteem, a possible binge eater with crazy food cravings which makes it hard to lose those last 10 to 20 pounds that never seem to come off.

Self-Sabotager:
Understands what it takes to be healthy but constantly has set backs and never reaches goals because of a lack of preparation, effort, motivation and willpower.

Healthy and Happy:
Fit, energetic, gets results and has strong will power when it comes to food and desires to take performance and energy to the next level, such as lowering body fat and increasing lean muscle mass.

Where are you on your journey?

No worries, I have been in all four stages during my health evolution and the key is to learn what works best for your body and lifestyle so you can progress.

All four stages have different needs and goals but it really comes down to two main issues. You must have greater hunger control, aka: will power, and make eating unhealthy foods a more difficult process. When you master these two critical steps, you will have more discipline with food, lose weight and getting healthier becomes an easier thing to do.

My first step is gaining greater hunger control, which means you naturally no longer have crazy cravings and food binge episodes. You are hungry less often, you have sustained energy levels. You have a higher metabolic rate. And fat starts to melt off of you.

My top three tips for great hunger control are:

- Eat only slow-acting carbs such as most vegetables, friendly fruits, quinoa, brown rice and rolled oats. These foods will maintain steady levels of glucose in your bloodstream and not spike blood sugar levels, leaving you satisfied for longer without the rollercoaster of cravings.
- Cut sugar. Foods loaded with sugar will spike your blood sugar and insulin levels leaving you super hungry with massive cravings shortly after you have eaten. The only okay natural sweetener I use is stevia!
- Add healthy fats to your diet. This has been my savior. To help reduce the edge from eliminating sugar from your diet and kill hunger, add healthy fats such as organic grass-fed butter, avocado, nuts, coconut oil, MCT oil and olive oil to your cooking and coffee. Healthy fats play a pivotal role in sending this important message to your brain: stop eating, you're full!

The second step to master is make eating unhealthy foods more difficult. When you make eating junk food difficult, you are more likely to break your bad eating habits. My top two tips for making junk food more difficult to eat are:

- Don't have any unhealthy foods accessible and in the house. The mind can only withstand so much. If it's easy to grab and in front of you then you are more likely to eat it because the body always wins. So clean out your kitchen and only allow healthy foods in your house.
- Every time you reach to eat bad foods, put a barrier between you and the food.

Choose Health Over Money - Managing a Stressful Job

Does your life include a sedentary job and stressful work environment?

After I graduated college, I took a corporate job as a mortgage banker. I quickly learned the pressures of a job in finance: deadlines, customer anxieties, corporate sales pressure, demanding real estate agents, government guidelines and laborious paperwork. The work took over and consumed my life.

I used to work 60-hour work weeks: late nights, taking work home, working on weekends, and when I wasn't working my mind was consumed with job stress. Then in 2008 on top of all the inherent job stress, the housing crisis hit and the banking industry got even more difficult with the failing economy. During weekdays I would hardly take breaks from behind the desk, grabbed whatever was convenient to eat, used food to cope with daily stress and was too drained after a long work day to get to the gym.

I had turned into a stressed-out, out-of-shape workaholic because of my sedentary and unhealthy work environment. Ultimately, I had chosen to live an unhealthy life for money. Yes, I was making six figures by the age of 27, but my body was paying the price.

I was at my heaviest, my marriage was on the rocks and I was on anti-anxiety pills because of the pressure. According to the American Psychological Association, most Americans are suffering from moderate to high stress, with 44 percent reporting that their stress levels have increased over the past five years. Concerns about money, work and the economy top the list of most frequently cited sources of stress.

I felt fat, unhealthy and gross in front of the mirror. My self-esteem was at an all-time low. Sure I was making great money but it wasn't worth the headache and heartache. At the time I didn't know what foods were toxic and bad for the body. I still had so much to learn.

I was getting more and more fed up with the way things were, as this version of my reality was not who I was meant to be. I was burnt out, disgusted with my body and my autoimmune issues were out of control. I had no natural energy, horrible mood swings and anxiety and was making me sick to my stomach with IBS (Irritable Bowel Syndrome). I knew something had to change.

You can eat, drink and do whatever you want to your body, but sooner or later, you will get a wake-up call about that reckless and thoughtless behavior. I wasn't taking care of myself. These struggles would become motivation for the new life I had to build.

As you begin to realize change as an opportunity for growth and newness, you bring to life the beauty of a brand new reality. When you take the courageous step to start listening and following your heart, you free yourself of the past and enter a fresh new chapter. I invite you to repeat the following healing mantra:

> As the master of my destiny and the creator of my reality, I accept the life that I thought I wanted does not represent the truth of who I am. I now realize I am not living my highest well-being. In knowing what I now know, I reclaim my health, allowing myself to express the divine light that I am. From this moment forward, I choose a new health-centered consciousness that heals and awakens all that I am. Prioritizing my mind, body and soul suggests how much better others deserve to treat themselves. When I exude health, I help inspire others by my presence.

Lesson #5: A sedentary and stressful life is guaranteed to give you an unhealthy body. Get active and reduce your stress for sustainable long-term health.

Love Yourself More - Dealing with Divorce

Have you ever been alone, brokenhearted and used drinking or emotional eating to cope?

According to divorcestatistics.org, 50% of all marriages in America end in divorce.

In 2009 I hit rock bottom. I was newly divorced, suffering with internal health issues and in a job that made me miserable. My marriage had fallen apart and I had lost someone who had promised me the world. I fell into a deep depression plagued with feelings of disappointment, betrayal and devastation. I cried myself to sleep every day for 8 months straight.

Divorce is brutal. Even when you know it's for the best to part ways, it's still one of the hardest things to go through. Instead of managing my stress in healthy ways, I indulged in unhealthy behaviors. To cope with the depression, I started drinking heavily and emotionally eating. I would pass out in the bathtub from my nightly therapy of wine combined with anti-anxiety pills, then wake up in a pool of cold water in the mornings. I felt frightened by myself and hated to be alone.

My emotional suffering triggered my binge eating episodes. In a recent study, two-fifths of Americans reported overeating or eating unhealthy foods because of stress. During my divorce I was comforted by alcohol, ice cream, pizza and whatever else would fill my emptiness. The recurring binge and/or purge cycles can affect the entire digestive system and can lead to electrolyte and chemical imbalances in the body that affect the heart and other major organ functions causing major health problems.

Due to my laxative abuse, I had chronic irregular bowel movements and constipation. To control the binge eating episodes this time, laxatives alone weren't enough so I incorporated enemas. Enemas provided quick relief to my food shaming and bloating problems. Self-destruction continued to rule my world.

I was officially broken--physically, mentally and emotionally. Life has a way of teaching you your own strength. I had to learn that I am perfectly capable of taking care of myself and that I am a strong independent woman.

If you find yourself hurt by someone you deeply love, you have the right to love yourself more than ever before. Surrender to your heart and please repeat this mantra with me:

> I freely give loving attention to whatever my body or mind calls out for. I forgive myself for any pain I may have caused myself. I give myself the tender loving care I deserve. I am capable of all things.

Lesson #6: You are your biggest supporter. In times of heartbreak you need more love, self-care and health not less.

Love Leads To Health - Single & Dating Advice

Do you ever engage in destructive and/or unhealthy behaviors hoping it will lead to love?

In my late twenties, I reentered the dating scene after 7 years of being in a relationship. As I have mentioned, up until this point I was using unhealthy measures to deal with my divorce. Even though I was still emotionally unstable from my divorce, it didn't stop me from dating again.

In my experience dating after divorce involved dining out, club-hopping, late-night drinking and drive-thru eating. To play the dating game involves losing your mind, blackout nights, party friends and wasting money on alcohol, Uber rides and over-priced restaurants.

One night when I was single and living in San Francisco, I specifically remember taking an Uber to my girlfriend's birthday party. Her party was at one of the hottest clubs in the city and she had a table with bottle service. I arrived at the club, poured myself a double vodka soda then continued to shake my booty on the dance floor.

It was close to 2 am and I was wasted. I could barely walk a straight line and was ready to go home. I texted Uber to come get me. On the way home, I made my Uber driver go through the Burger King drive-thru for a late-night junk food binge. I got home to my studio, stuffed my face and passed out.

The next morning I woke up completely hungover to two enemy cheeseburger wrappers and fries. I felt like death. I was still bloated from the night before so I went to the bathroom and gave myself an enema to alleviate my pain, as it was getting harder and harder to go to the bathroom on my own. I was officially dependent on enemas and had almost destroyed my digestive system. I still felt like crap, went back to bed and didn't wake up until 6 pm. that night.

This became a regular party-going habit for me with my party-going friends. I still hadn't cleaned up my act. I knew deep down it was time to stop the drinking and partying as it was fueling the fire of my unhealthy eating habits. It is common for eating disorders to occur with alcohol and other substance abuse. So I decided to give myself a 30-Day No Drinking Challenge and step away from my party friends because my world had become too toxic.

Two to three days into my cleanse, a guy I was dating texted me to see if I wanted to grab a glass of wine. I politely declined and explained to him I wasn't drinking for 30 days. He said, "Oh okay. Good luck with that." There was no alternative date suggestion that didn't involve alcohol or emotional encouragement. Needless to say, I never spoke to that man again.

When a guy doesn't try to understand you, never calls and would rather text, these are alarming signs you could be getting played.

In my experience, that's the game some guys would play. Get girls drunk then they are easier targets to manipulate and get physical. I could see through this game and decided I was no longer participating. Any man who is truly interested and respects you as a woman doesn't want to manipulate you with fancy dinners or alcohol. He wants to listen and get to know who you are sober, with both ears and an open heart. He tries to understand you: your thoughts, how you feel and what makes you tick. This realization was the turning point in my health evolution.

It only helps you to act on love. It is your willingness to only accept love and support from yourself and others that allows your heart to open. Love is the answer and the only reality. Please repeat the following healing mantra:

> I accept love as my greatest ally, love's only purpose is to heal me on my health journey. I choose love. I promise to protect my body and soul with loving and healthy choices.

Lesson #7: *True love leads you to health. If a friend or a man doesn't treat you with the highest respect and support your healthy decisions then he or she doesn't deserve to be in your life.*

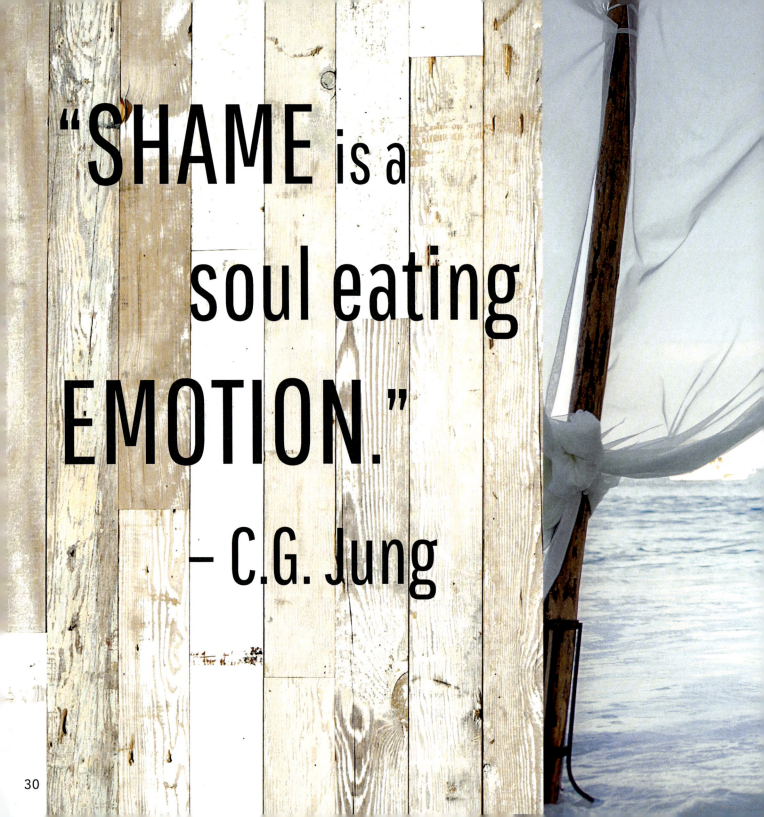

THE RISE
PART 2

Josafat de la Toba

Angels Appear - The Universe Is Working In Your Favor

Have you ever noticed that no matter what you have been through, there is always another chance around the corner?

I was finally cleaning up my life, having real discipline and going for goals in a bigger way than ever before. I was building confidence, getting healthy and having success. By 2011, I had left my miserable mortgage job, started following my heart and reinvented my career.

I created a healthy living blog, called beautybreakthru.com, to help women with the struggles I had been through. I had found a new purpose in life. While doing research for my blog, I met my now business partner and best friend, Emily. She introduced me to an incredible health and wellness company that offers organic supplements, that along with a healthy diet and lifestyle, helped me eliminate my digestive issues and stop my dependence on enemas. Emily was an answer to my prayers and I am grateful for her every day.

Life was turning around. I had finally met a friend who truly cared about helping me live a healthier life and I was having online success with my blog. I was living in San Francisco at the time and decided to attend a business seminar in Los Angeles called the Personal Story Power Event, given by ex NFL player and public speaker Bo Eason.

At the event, I met my husband Todd. He was working at the event and it was love at first sight. From the moment we first spoke there was an electric connection, something beyond this world. I remember it so vividly. I was sitting in the attendance crowd and the DJ setup was in the back right corner of the room. I glanced over and saw this super hot guy behind the table playing the music. A new song came on that I didn't know the name of and I wanted to download it.

So I approached him and asked, "Hey, what's the name of this song so I can download it for my iTunes?" Todd went to check his computer for the name of the song and suddenly all of his equipment shut off. Very smoothly I said, "That's our electric connection that shut the computer down." I started flirting. :) He said "No, I have a short in my cable."

He then checked the cable wire and started to play along with me. "OH WOW, there is no short, you must be right," Todd said. He told me the name of the song, I thanked him and went back to my seat.

The whole day I could feel him vibing on me, checking me out. After the day was over, I went back over to him and we exchanged information. After the event we started dating. I told him about my past struggles and the blog I was building. Todd was supportive from day one. He quickly jumped on board, not only helping me build my business, but also with my commitment to personal health.

Todd became my accountability buddy. In my moments of weakness and when faced with food temptations that would trigger my binge eating episodes, such as alcohol, desserts, pastas and breads, he was right there to lovingly remind me of my health goals and past habits. At the right moments, he gave me the strength and discipline I needed to overcome my food obsessions. Today we are each other's biggest supporters in business and health. I am so lucky.

Our electricity still sparks hot to this day. I am forever grateful that the stars aligned to allow our paths to cross. Todd has helped me pursue my dreams, build my confidence and ultimately become the woman I am today. The days of being with selfish, toxic and egotistical men are over. Please repeat the following healing mantra:

> I am perfect in every way. No matter what has happened in the past, love is always there to find me.

Lesson #8: *The universe responds to choices. When you start making healthier choices, good people and things come into your life. True love is based on a soulful connection of encouragement, generosity, kindness and selflessness.*

No More Guilt - Getting Over Food Shaming

How often do you feel guilty about the foods you eat?

We live in a guilt-based society. As individuals we internalize our society's idea of what's beautiful and sexy and what's not. We don't need anyone to punish our behaviors because we are the first to punish ourselves. Therefore, we always feel guilty and pressured by societal images to be perfect, young, wealthy and thin. Perpetuated by ads and consumerism, Victoria's Secret models, and, yes, the use of Photoshop, these unrealistic body images are constantly sold to us as what is considered desirable.

You may desire to be younger, thinner or sexier but all you really need is a healthy mind that is understanding, compassionate and conscious. The rest will follow.

As a healthy lifestyle expert, I have noticed how often the women I work with beat themselves up over the the food they eat. They feel so guilty when they get off track with their diets and cheat with wine, ice cream, pizza, etc...anything they know they shouldn't be eating because it is slowing their weight loss.

I can relate. I used to be stuck in a negative cycle of emotions when it comes to food shaming. Todd and I had been dating for almost a year when my parents took us to Playa del Carmen, Mexico for Christmas in 2012. We stayed at the most beautiful resort called Blue Diamond. Blue Diamond is an all-inclusive resort where you get a wristband and can eat and drink as much as you want!

It was a recovering binge eater's dream and worst nightmare at the same time. We felt like kids at Christmas. We ate our faces off: breakfast buffet, all-you-can-eat sushi by the pool, frozen umbrella drinks and tequila shots, pizza, delicious Mexican food, multiple entrees and desserts every night for dinner. We went overboard!

We were at Blue Diamond for a week. When we got back home to LA we weighed ourselves (I know bad idea, lol). We both had gained 10 pounds in a week! We felt so bad about ourselves, beating ourselves up to the max. We vowed to never go back to fat camp again on a vacation.

Our next vacations were to the Caribbean and back down to Cabo. We still enjoyed ourselves by eating whatever we wanted but incorporated exercise during the day to add back that healthy balance.

My point is if you choose to give yourself a break from healthy eating, such as being on vacation or taking the day off from your diet, then enjoy yourself. Love yourself for giving yourself the luxury to eat whatever you want. Choose to see it as a reward not as if you are cheating yourself. It's ok to NOT be perfect 100% of the time on your diet because at any moment you can choose to be healthy again. This mentality will keep you sane and stop you from driving yourself crazy.

I recommend one meal or day per week that is a reward, where you can eat whatever you want. It's all about balance, sustainability and not going insane. You don't have to be a drill sergeant when it comes to healthy eating to lose weight. When you eat something bad there is no punishment. Being healthy is about flexibility and balance along with treating yourself right both physically and mentally.

Simply by giving yourself a break when it comes to diet and healthy eating, you cultivate an ability to feel guiltless and happy about all foods you eat. Please repeat the following healing mantra:

> I am powerful. I love and reward myself shamelessly.

Lesson #9: At any moment, you can choose to feel good about what you eat, yourself and your health.

> "We ate our faces off: breakfast buffet, all-you can-eat sushi by the pool, frozen umbrella drinks and tequilla shots, pizza, delicous Mexican food, multiple entrees and desserts every night for dinner. We went overboard!"

Losing Weight With Ease - Mastering The Process

Do you make yourself miserable to be thin?

I had now stabilized my binge eating episodes with the support of friends and family, discovered new organic products and was learning how nutritiously dense foods drench our cells with the vitamins and minerals our bodies need to satisfy hunger.

However, I still didn't realize that gluten and sugar cause inflammation in the body and that inflammation makes losing weight virtually impossible. I thought I was eating relatively healthy at the time. But gluten and naturally occurring sugar found in foods like bananas, granola, sweetened milks, artifical sugars and dates were still part of my daily diet.

So with the presence sugar and gluten working against my body, to meet my weight loss goals I used to slave away on the treadmill, do extreme calorie restriction and nutritional deprivation through juice cleansing rather than diet pills, enemas and laxatives.

I do believe that intermittent fasting for 12 to 16 hours is effective for fat burning without strongly affecting moods and sanity. However, my cleansing at the time consisted of weekly 72-hour juicing cycles, leaving my moods on edge and urges to poke my husband's eyes out. The combination of extreme cardio--running 5 miles, 4 days per week, plus cycle class 2 days a week--and regular weekly cleansing did indeed help me reach my weight loss goal of 120 pounds. But the reality is, it is NOT a sustainable weight loss plan especially for how active of a person I am and made the process miserable. Therefore, I quickly burnt out physically along with having emotional breakdowns.

Fast-forward a couple months later to September of 2014 when I couldn't get out of bed for 3 straight days...I didn't have the flu, a fever or a cold. I had no energy and felt like I had been hit by a truck, something was definitely wrong.

After 3 days straight of sleeping, I conjured up some energy to get dressed and headed to the doctor. My doctor took blood and I was diagnosed with Hashimoto's Thyroiditis, a disorder in which the immune system turns against the body's own tissues and attacks the thyroid.

The American Thyroid Association reported that an estimated 20 million Americans have some form of thyroid disease. Women are 5 to 8 times more likely than men to have thyroid problems. And 1 woman in 8 will develop a thyroid disorder during her lifetime.

I discovered the food I was eating was contributing to my autoimmune disease struggles and making weight loss a battle I was losing. I dove deep into research about how to balance my thyroid so I could regain my energy and vitality.

What I found is balancing your thyroid takes consistent effort and energy. There are crucial things you can do to stabilize the tiredness, crazy moods, hair loss, fatigue, weight gain and stress that come with thyroid suffering. Autoimmune Thyroid Disease (AITD) is caused by a litany of toxic factors.

In my case, I needed to cleanse my body of gluten. What explains the connection? It's a case of mistaken identity. The molecular structure of gliadin, the protein portion of gluten, closely resembles that of the thyroid gland. When gliadin breaches the protective barrier of the gut, and enters the bloodstream, the immune system tags it for destruction. These antibodies to gliadin also cause the body to attack thyroid tissue. This means if you have AITD and you eat foods containing gluten, your immune system will attack your thyroid.

Also, data suggests that certain carbs, especially inflammatory carbs like gluten, cause insulin spikes. Overproduction of insulin causes your body to store fat and stored fat promotes inflammation in the body. Chronic inflammation is a hallmark of disease, ranging from damage to arteries, cancer, and a decreased immune system from foods.

My doctor put me on a thyroid hormone replacement pill but I still wasn't feeling any better. So I decided to check out other options and went to see a naturopath. I got screened for food allergies and intolerances, hormone imbalances, toxicity and other internal issues. My naturopath found I had an overgrowth of candida, which is essentially an overproduction of yeast in the body due to sugar causing inflammation overload.

The candida overgrowth had zapped my natural energy, inflamed my entire endocrine system and was spiking my insulin levels, which aided the attack against my thyroid gland. There are more than 70 health disorders that are connected to sugar consumption. Some of the most common include: diabetes, lack of concentration, obesity, allergies, asthma, ADHD, hypoglycemia, mood swings, immune and nutritional deficiencies. I knew at that moment, sugar was my enemy and I had to give it up.

Chronic inflammation leads to disease, sickness and shortening of life. To reduce the inflammation in my body, the plan was to reduce the amount of toxicity and stress by: cutting out sugar, gluten, and pesticide-grown, non-organic foods, as well as reducing emotional stress.

I no longer wanted to be a cardio queen and deprive myself of food for days to be thin. I knew I had to quit gluten and sugar to get my health and sanity back. I was on a mission to healthfully sustain my body goals, regain health and balanced my thyroid.

Your perfect health is waiting for you. I offer you relief from any physical pain, discomfort and suffering. To experience freedom from any health challenges, please repeat the following healing mantra:

> No matter what I am dealing with big or small; I am strong, healthy and whole. I choose to clear and release any toxins, inflammation and disease from my body in an attempt to live a long and healthy life. I promise to make healthy choices from a place of love and will of my highest well-being through my reclaimed power.

Lesson #10: Losing weight with ease is a reality when you reduce inflammation in the body by eliminating gluten and sugar. Then there is no need for extreme calorie deprivation and cardio overkill.

Food Rehab - Quitting Sugar & Gluten

Based on my own personal experience and those I have worked with, I see two types of food addicts:

First are the *sugar addicts* who think they eat healthy but their diets are filled with hidden sugars in foods such as granolas, unfriendly fruits, alcohol and foods naturally high in sugar that cause inflammation in their bodies. They are always frustrated because they can never lose the weight they desire to come off. They are addicted to sugar and don't even know it.

Second are the *carb lovers* who cannot refrain from eating breads, sandwiches, pizza and pastas. They need to eat carbs in moderation, including only healthier non-inflammatory alternatives, and reduce portion size so they can meet their goals.

Are you one of these addicts? I know how crazy food cravings can be. Here are my *7 Steps On How To Stop Food Addictions* that may be ruining your body and life:

1. **Cut all sugar out of your diet.** Foods loaded with sugar will spike your blood sugar and insulin levels leaving you super hungry with massive cravings shortly after you have eaten. The only okay natural sweetener I recommend is stevia.

2. **Eat more healthy fats.** When I quit sugar, adding more healthy fats to my diet was my savior. Increasing healthy fats helps to reduce the edge from eliminating sugar from your diet and kills hunger. Healthy fats play a pivotal role in sending this important message to your brain: stop eating, you're full! All the recipes in this book are designed specifically to maximize your hunger control.

3. **Eat only slow-acting and non-inflammatory carbs** and vegetables, which are listed on the Healthy Kitchen Pantry and Grocery Lists on pages 48-50. These foods will maintain steady levels of glucose in your bloodstream and not spike blood sugar levels, leaving you satisfied for longer without the rollercoaster of cravings.

4. **Drink at least a gallon of water per day** to cleanse and purge the body. Increase your H2O intake by squeezing fresh lemons into your water (this helps alkalize your body), carry a refillable water bottle around with you at all times and 10 minutes before eating a meal, or even a small snack, drink a full glass of water.

5. **Clean out your kitchen.** Throw away any unhealthy foods such as: processed, high-sugar breads, pasta, chips and cereals, white bread or bagels, corn flakes, puffed rice, bran flakes, instant oatmeal, white rice, rice pasta, macaroni and cheese, pumpkin pretzels, rice cakes, popcorn and saltine crackers.

Then only allow friendly foods in your house as I mention in the Cooking Preparation Section on page 47.

6. **Start reading labels** and do not eat anything with: sugar alcohol, gluten, sugar, wheat, soy, honey, agave, maple syrup, dried fruits, high fructose corn syrup, enriched flour and corn sweetener, etc.

7. **Eat healthy sweet tooth substitutions** when feeling a sweet craving with any of my Guilt-Free Desserts starting on page 161.

Love What You See In The Mirror - Overcoming Body Shaming

Do you ever look in the mirror and feel disgusted with yourself?

Not so long ago, I used to stand in front of the mirror naked and pick out, pinch and obsess over the areas of my body I thought were ugly. For me, I hated my legs and butt because of the cellulite. I yearned for toned, lean and cellulite-free legs. I never wanted to wears shorts because I was so ashamed and afraid to show others my fatty legs.

Eighty percent of women have admitted the mirror makes them feel bad. A recent survey of 5,000 women, commissioned by REAL magazine, found that 91% of women were unhappy with their hips and thighs, 77% were dissatisfied with their waist and 78% said they had cellulite.

I started doing research on cellulite and what I learned is it's not a flaw. Cellulite is a normal function of the way women's bodies store fat. Eighty to ninety percent of women have cellulite to some degree. Even though I learned that most women have cellulite, that didn't make me feel any better about myself when I looked in the mirror at my naked behind.

As I mentioned before, I knew I had to quit sugar and gluten due to my thyroid. So now was the time. I gave myself a *30-Day No Sugar or Gluten Challenge*. A strong woman doesn't shy away from challenge, she says bring it on! This challenge included no bread, pastas, pizza, or inflammatory carbs…and no added sugar, artificial or natural sugars such as cereals, protein bars, fruit unfriendly fruits, dates, honey, alcohol, maple syrup, agave, etc.

The first two weeks were the worst. I had crazy sugar cravings and all my body wanted was sweets. The worst was late-night cravings around 9 or 10 pm so I would go for herbal tea with a splash of unsweetened organic almond milk to subside the urge. Did you know that according to brain scans sugar is as addictive as cocaine? Well, I was fully addicted and kicking the habit was tougher than I expected.

I pushed through and completed the challenge! I felt so amazing, proud and my natural energy had returned. I felt like a new woman. There was no way I was going back. I kept going with the no sugar and gluten. The best part is, after a few months, I started to see a reduction in my cellulite!

Quitting sugar and gluten helped me reduce my cellulite insecurity. It didn't get rid of it all but it made a big enough difference that when I looked in the mirror I didn't feel so bad about it. If you are like me and cellulite really bothers you then I suggest you quit sugar and gluten and see the difference for yourself.

Taking on the *30-Day No Sugar or Gluten Challenge* can only help your internal health and external body confidence. Go for it, you have nothing to lose but cellulite! You are beautiful no matter what. Please repeat the following healing mantra:

> No matter how I feel, I am here every minute, hour, day, month and year to give myself the love, health and confidence I deserve. I am my own strength.

Lesson #11: Believe your body is beautiful, it's not about perfection but progress.

"i BELIEVE that the greatest GIFT you can give your FAMILY and the world is a HEALTHY YOU." - Joyce Meyer

THE TRIUMPH
PART 3

Super Fit and Sane - Finding Your Happy Place

What's the biggest accomplishment of your life?

I hear the trumpets blowing! I recently turned 34 years old and I have never felt or looked better in my life! For me, this is one of my life's biggest accomplishment as I have overcome poor digestion, depression, anxiety, overeating, up-and-down weight gain, an eating disorder, sugar addiction, body image and autoimmune issues to get to a place of self-love and total health.

I tear up writing this to you as I realize it has been an 18-year chaotic battle for my health, happiness and sanity. It's been brutal but I am stronger, smarter and wiser for experiencing it. I am proud to say I have successfully quit sugar, gluten, drugs, diet pills, laxatives, enemas, participating in toxic relationships, starving and torturing myself. The days of self-shaming and pain are over. Thank you God!

However, my greatest success so far in life is I have won the battle against all my deepest fears, body insecurities, self-doubt, inner health, will power and emotional issues. What I know for sure is: self-abuse, body obsession, eating struggles and poor health leads to transformation and your highest well-being.

Of course there are days when I am not 100% perfect and that's okay. The good news is I know how to immediately get back on track because, remember, at any moment we can choose to be healthy again. Everything you need to know about how to get back on track with your goals and exactly what to do is in this book.

Eighty-five percent of the world's population is affected by low self-esteem. My hope is that if you struggle, like I did, then I pray your tribulations end sooner than 18 years of suffering. So please implement my strategies, recipes, mantras, wisdom and eating plans to see if it makes a difference in your life, as you have nothing to lose and only happiness to gain. I want nothing but the best for you. For those of you who are knee-deep in eating struggles, yearning to break through to the other side, I offer you everything in this book. Please repeat the following healing mantra:

> I am successful. I am resilient. I am loved and I am free.

Lesson #12: Total body success is knowing how to eat right, having discipline and making healthy choices enjoyable.

My Gift of Health Evolution

Do you feel motivated, fit and strong?

I once was lost in reckless unhealthy behaviors that manifested in much suffering but now I am healthy and free. I had to get radically honest, face my destructive habits and start loving myself. Today it's my personal promise to always protect and prevent myself from poor health so I can be strong, energetic, productive and happy. I call it wearing *awesome armor*.

I offer you health evolution statements with love and support to your heart as part of your healing journey. As your heart opens up it will ensure your growth and evolution. As a way of discovering the love you have always wanted to hear or never heard often enough, please repeat the following phrases:

> I am open to receive all the health, love and kindness I deserve.
> There is nothing wrong with me.
> I am precious.
> I love the part of me who so desperately wants to be loved even when others treat me poorly.
> No one can hurt me.
> I am unbreakable.
> I do the best I can.
> I always have an opportunity to be healthy.
> I am so grateful to receive the support I need to end my struggles.
> I forgive myself.
> I choose love.
> I promise to protect my body and soul with healthy choices.
> I am perfect in every way.
> No matter what has happened in the past, love is always there.
> I am powerful.
> I love myself.
> No matter what I am dealing with big or small; I am strong.
> No matter how I feel; I am here every second, minute, hour, day, month and year to love myself.
> I am successful.
> I am free of pain.

I hope this book helps you find the motivation to love yourself more than ever before so your body can be as strong as possible. Please use all my wisdom as your *awesome armor* too!

If you follow my teachings, I promise you will see weight loss results and have all the naked confidence you desire. If you love yourself more, not less, eat right and live a healthy lifestyle then you will become invincible. Never forget how special you truly are.

Now is the time to get started: set yourself up for success, make a commitment and stick to a my *Naked Confidence Eating Plans* (see page 54). Be proud and love your life!

Cooking Preparation Steps

Learn How To Cook Healthy & Make Weight Loss Easy

1. Kitchen Clean-Out, Throw It Away!!!

The first step is to make eating unhealthy foods more difficult by doing a kitchen clean-out. This means DO NOT have any unhealthy foods accessible in the house. The mind can only withstand so much and if it's easy, you are more likely to eat it because the body always wins. So clean out your kitchen and only allow healthy foods in your house.

Rid your pantry, fridge, and freezer of any unhealthy junk foods such as: white foods, breads, pasta, soda, ice cream, chips, etc., so you can make room for the nutritious foods.

2. Shop Healthy & Organic

When you are out shopping, buy free-range turkey and chicken, grass-fed beef and butter and organic produce when you can.
- Why buy organic? Opting for organic foods is a smarter choice for personal and planetary health because they are free of harmful chemicals, more nutritionally dense, taste better, reduce environmental pollution, you avoid hormones in animal products that have been directly linked to cancer and keep our families safe.
- Why buy free-range? Choosing to buy free-range chicken, eggs and turkey is the simplest thing you can do to help the animals have access to the outdoors and not be confined in cages. Cages confine hens, providing little space for the hens' ability to carry out natural behaviors such as walking, wing-flapping, perching and nesting. You are contributing to increased animal welfare.
- Why buy grass-fed? Grass-fed beats grain-fed because it offers lower levels of unhealthy fats, higher levels of omega-3 fatty acids, lower levels of cholesterol and twice the amount of conjugated linoleic acid, which may have cancer-fighting properties, lower the risk of diabetes and other health problems.

3. Set Yourself Up for Success

Setting yourself up for success starts by stocking your kitchen with healthy foods and ingredients that are conducive to weight loss and only allowing those items in your home.

Healthy Kitchen Pantry Checklist

Non-Inflammatory Slow-Acting Carbs
- [ ] Gluten-Free Rolled Oats
- [ ] Quinoa
- [ ] Brown Rice

Oils & Healthy Fats
- [ ] Extra Virgin Olive Oil
- [ ] MCT Oil
- [ ] Coconut Oil
- [ ] Sesame Oil
- [ ] Raw Almond Butter
- [ ] Grass-Fed Butter
- [ ] Can of Coconut Cream
- [ ] Organic Peanut Butter

Nuts & Seeds
- [ ] Chia Seeds
- [ ] Raw Almonds
- [ ] Raw Walnuts
- [ ] Pistachios
- [ ] Raw Macadamia
- [ ] Raw Cashews
- [ ] Pecans

Protein & SuperFoods
(Found at your local organic food store and/or online)
- [ ] Undenatured Vanilla and Chocolate Whey or Vegan Protein Powders
- [ ] Organic Cacao Powder
- [ ] Maca Powder

Seasonings & Spices
- [ ] Cayenne Pepper
- [ ] Garlic Powder
- [ ] Cinnamon
- [ ] Stevia
- [ ] Pink Himalayan Salt
- [ ] Black Pepper
- [ ] Organic Vegetable Stock
- [ ] Dried Thyme
- [ ] Minced Garlic
- [ ] Organic Vanilla Extract
- [ ] Organic Vanilla Powder
- [ ] Braggs Amino Acids
- [ ] Cilantro
- [ ] Ginger Powder
- [ ] Cumin
- [ ] Curry Powder
- [ ] Dried Parsley
- [ ] Balsamic Vinegar
- [ ] Red Wine Vinegar
- [ ] Paprika
- [ ] All spice

Beverages
- [ ] Organic Coffee
- [ ] Almond Milk, Organic & Unsweetened
- [ ] Coconut Milk, Organic & Unsweeted
- [ ] Filtered Water

Baking
- [ ] Almond Meal
- [ ] Coconut Flour
- [ ] Coconut Palm Sugar
- [ ] At Least 70% Cacao Dark Chocolate Bars
- [ ] Shredded Coconut

Condiments
- [ ] Dijon Mustard
- [ ] Hot Sauce
- [ ] No Sugar Added Ketchup

Equipment Checklist - Tools You Need!
- [ ] Blender - I love the Ninja Blender Duo, buy at ninjakitchen.com
- [ ] Spiralizer
- [ ] Food Processor

Friendly Foods Grocery List
Foods That Contribute To Weight Loss

Fruits
Apples
Strawberries
Blueberries
Lemons
Oranges
Limes

Milk Alternatives
Coconut Milk
Almond Milk

Starches
Butternut Squash
*All Slow-Acting Carbs, see page 48

Organic Vegetables
Mushrooms
Broccoli
Spinach
Kale
Cucumber
Tomato
Avocado
Celery
Zucchini
Onion
Asparagus
Cauliflower
Chives
Bell peppers
Arugula
Romaine

Fresh Herbs
Ginger root
Cilantro
Rosemary
Parsley

Protein
Wild Salmon
Grass-Fed Beef
Bison Burger
Nitrate-Free Bacon
Tilapia
Free-Range Chicken
Organic Eggs
Shrimp

OK Dairy
Grass-Fed Butter
Shredded Parmesan
Feta
Goat Cheese

Killer Foods
Unfriendly Foods That Slow & Stop Weight Loss

AVOID AT ALL COSTS
- soda
- alcohol
- fast food
- fried foods
- white foods
- processed foods (anything that comes packaged and frozen)
- limited dairy except select items listed on the friendly foods list
- soy
- refined white sugars, artificial sweeteners, sugar-free, sugar alcohol, corn syrup, agave, maple syrup, dried fruits, honey, dates, unfriendly fruits (any fruit not on the friendly foods list), alcohol and/or added sugars.
- bread or pasta

Rules To Live By

When in doubt, throw it out.

If it's green, you'll grow lean.

If it's brown, slow down.

If you stray, get back on track the next day.

Retreat from sweets.

If it's white, keep it out of sight.

Sweat after starches.

NAKED CONFIDENCE
EATING PLANS

Getting Started Eating Plan

How Much To Eat:
Use this as a daily guide for diet ratios, eat until you are full.
Oil & Healthy Fats - 5-9 servings
Fruit, Starch or Carbs - 1 servings
Organic Veggies - 6-11 servings
Protein - 4-6 servings

When & What To Eat:
Monday - Friday
Breakfast (7am-10am):
Super Coffee (see page, 61)
Green Smoothie or Protein Shake
Option (see pages, 77-94)

Post-Workout/Lunch (10am-2pm):
Protein Shake, Power Salad, Soulful
Soup or Bunless Burger Option
(see pages, 85-118)

Afternoon Snack (2pm-5pm):
Healthy Snack Option
(see pages, 119-126)

Dinner (5pm-8pm):
Divine Dinner Option
(see pages, 127-152)

Dessert if Desired (8pm):
Guilt-Free Dessert Option
(see pages, 161-172)

Saturday
Wake Up (7am-9am):
Super Coffee (see page, 61)

Brunch (9am-1pm):
Eggs & More or Lunch Option
(see pages, 59-76 and 95-118)

Afternoon Snack (1pm-5pm):
Healthy Snack Option
(see pages, 119-126)

Dinner (5pm-8pm):
Grill It Up Option
(see pages, 143-152)

Dessert if Desired (8pm):
Guilt-Free Dessert Option
(see pages, 161-172)

Sunday
Wake Up (7am-9am):
Super Coffee (see page, 61)

Brunch (9am-1pm):
Eggs & More or Lunch Option
(see pages, 59-76 and 95-118)

Afternoon Snack (1pm-5pm):
Healthy Snack Option
(see pages, 119-126)

Dinner (5pm-8pm):
Divine Dinner Option
(see pages, 127-152)

Dessert if Desired (8pm):
Guilt-Free Dessert Option
(see pages, 161-172)

Fat Melting Eating Plan

How Much To Eat:
Cut Your 1 Serving of Fruit, Starch or Carbs &
Increase 1-2 Servings of Oil and Healthy Fats
(from the Getting Started Plan)

When & What To Eat:
Monday - Sunday
Morning (6am-noon):
Super Coffee (see page, 61)

Post-Workout/Lunch (Noon-2pm):
Protein Shake, Power Salad, Soulful Soup or Bunless Burger Option
(see pages, 85-118)

Afternoon Snack (2pm-5pm):
Healthy Snack and/or Green Smoothie Option (see pages, 77-84 and 119-126)

Dinner (5pm-8pm):
Divine Dinner Option (see pages, 127-152)

Dessert (8pm):
If you absolutely need something sweet have 1 square of at least 70% cacao dark chocolate.

*Allow yourself one reward meal per week where you eat whatever you want for both eating plans! Usually I have my reward meal Friday night!

*This fat-melting eating plan is an intermittent fasting strategy. Under this plan you fast for 16 hours, which means you will NOT eat between 8pm and noon the next day. Most of your fast occurs while you are sleeping. Skip breakfast in the morning and wait until noon to eat your recommended servings. This is an 8-hour feeding window and referred to as the 16/8 fasting protocol. Repeat this pattern every day.

What To Expect:

What is your why?

First, take a moment to be mindful of your motivations. Why are making these new healthy changes important to you? Write them down and post them somewhere visible so you don't lose sight of what you want!

The most successful people in this world attach meaning to everything they do, they know exactly who they are and what drives them. Discovering what drives you, or your "Why," is important. Make sure you attach a strong "Why" to your goals that will clearly and powerfully help you push through times of weakness and guide you to your highest well-being.

If you are a sugar addict or eat processed and refined foods, you may begin to experience some withdrawal symptoms. This is definitely normal to feel and it will most likely subside over the first couple weeks.

As your body continues to eliminate toxins that you have accumulated, you will begin to regain more of your natural energy. If you keep struggling with sugar cravings and bad eating habits then see page 38 for steps on how to give yourself a food rehab.

You'll quickly see how eating healthy nutritious foods can transform your energy level, sleep patterns, and daily discomforts. My recipes will increase your energy, heal your digestion and boost your metabolism so you can start losing weight and living better. Now start cooking!!

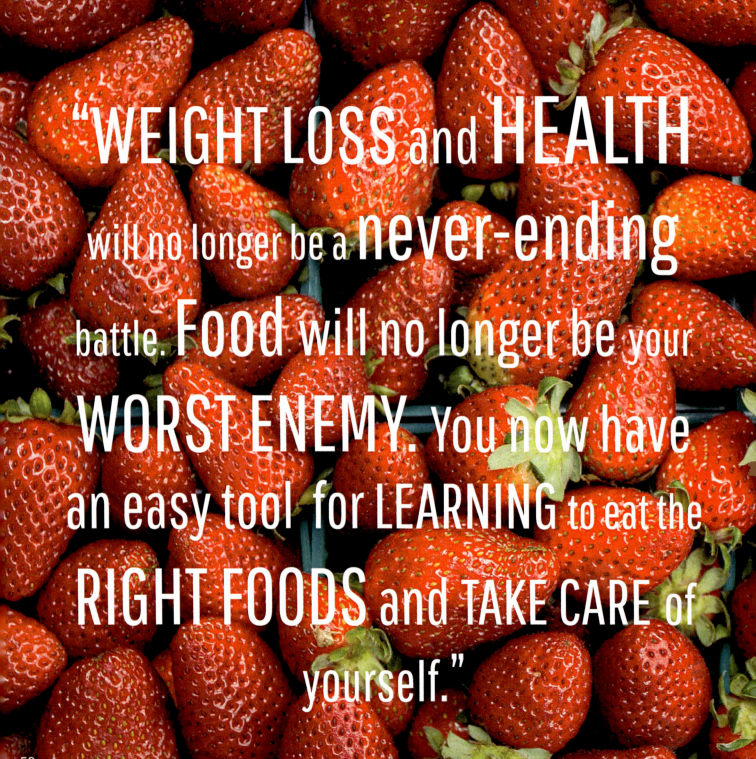

"WEIGHT LOSS and HEALTH will no longer be a never-ending battle. Food will no longer be your WORST ENEMY. You now have an easy tool for LEARNING to eat the RIGHT FOODS and TAKE CARE of yourself."

RECIPES

All recipes are non-inflammatory, gluten-free, soy-free and unrefined.

BREAKFAST

Super Coffee
Serves 1

Super charge your mind and body with this energy booster, not your ordinary cup of coffee.

Ingredients
- 8-ounces of organic fresh brewed coffee
- ¼ teaspoon MCT oil or coconut oil
- ½ teaspoon grass-fed butter

Directions
Combine coffee, oil and butter in blender. Once mixed frothy, drink and enjoy.

*Inspired by Bulletproof Coffee

> "You have two options: keep getting sicker and living miserably, or do everything you can to feel better and enjoy your life."

EGGS & MORE

Tomato Feta Scramble
Serves 4-6

This simple and delicious breakfast is quick enough for any day of the week.

Ingredients
- ½ cup ripe tomatoes, chopped
- ½ cup feta cheese
- ½ cup fresh arugula
- pinch of salt
- pinch of black pepper
- 1 tablespoon extra virgin oil olive
- 2 cups of egg whites

Directions
Place the egg whites, tomato, feta, salt and pepper into the a blender. Pulse until all ingredients are roughly chopped.

In a medium saute pan add the oil, egg mixture and arugula then cook over medium heat, stirring frequently until cooked through.

Mushroom + Artichoke Scramble
Serves 4-6

This quick breakfast will leave you satisfied and ready for the day!

Ingredients
- ½ cup white mushrooms, sliced
- ½ cup parmesan cheese
- ½ cup fresh artichokes
- pinch of salt
- pinch of black pepper
- 1 tablespoon extra virgin oil olive
- 2 cups of egg whites

Directions
Place the egg whites, artichokes, parmesan, mushrooms, salt and pepper into the a blender. Pulse until all ingredients are roughly chopped.

In a medium saute pan add the oil and egg mixture then cook over medium heat, stirring frequently and scramble until cooked through.

OMG Scramble
Serves 4-6

This breakfast scramble will rock your world with delight!

Ingredients
- ½ cup white mushrooms, sliced
- ½ cup parmesan cheese
- ½ cup onion, chopped
- ½ cup spinach
- ½ cup bacon, chopped
- stevia
- pinch of salt
- pinch of black pepper
- 1 tablespoon coconut or MCT oil
- 2 cups of egg whites

Directions
In a large pan add oil, onion and bacon then sprinkle with stevia and cook over medium heat, stirring frequently until cooked through.

Place the egg whites, parmesan, mushrooms, salt and pepper into the a blender. Pulse until all ingredients are roughly chopped.

Add the egg mixture and spinach to the pan with the cooked bacon, stirring frequently until cooked through together.

Protein Scramble
Serves 1-2

This low carb protein packed breakfast that will get you energized for the day.

Ingredients
- 1/2 chicken breast cut into small cubes
- 3 egg whites
- ¼ cup mushrooms
- ¼ cup spinach
- salt & pepper to taste
- 1 tablespoon of olive olive

Directions
Heat a medium saute pan, add oil over medium heat. Saute chicken for 3 minutes, add mushrooms and spinach. Cook for another 5 minutes until chicken has golden color. Add salt and pepper to your taste.

Add egg whites and scramble all ingredient together.

*Tastes great topped with hot sauce!

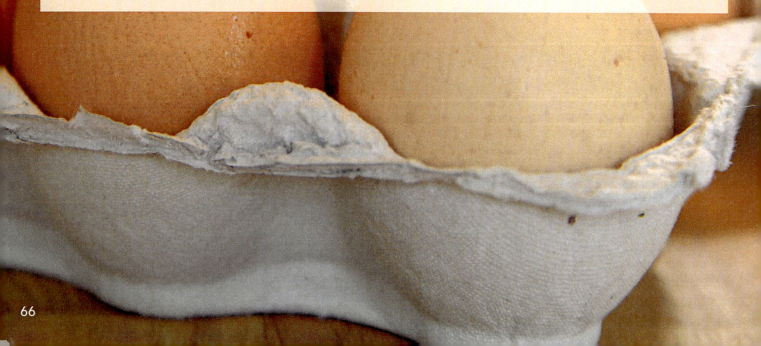

Salmon Benedict
Serves 1

A tasty and healthy gourmet breakfast to try to liven up your morning.

Ingredients
- 4-ounces of wild salmon
- 1 whole organic egg
- ¼ cup spinach
- salt and pepper to taste
- 1 tablespoon coconut or MCT oil
- 1 teaspoon extra virgin olive oil
- 1 avocado, sliced

Directions
Pre-heat oven to 325 degrees Fahrenheit.

Rub salmon with coconut or mct oil and put in oven for 8 to 12 minutes or until desired degree of doneness in a baking pan.

Boil 4 cups of water, add whole egg to water. Boil for 45 seconds to a minute. Use perforated spoon to pull the egg out.

Saute spinach in olive oil for 3 minutes. Place spinach first on plate, then put the salmon on top of the spinach. Garnish on top with the poached egg. Put a pinch of black pepper on top of the poached egg with slices of avocado.

Lobster + Asparagus Frittata
Serves 4-6

This italian dish is an equally efficient and delicious breakfast, perfect for brunch!!

Ingredients
- 6 whole eggs
- 3 egg whites
- ½ teaspoon salt
- ¼ teaspoon black pepper
- 2 teaspoons extra virgin olive oil
- 1 cup onion, chopped
- ½ cup red bell pepper, chopped
- 1 teaspoon dried oregano
- 8-ounces asparagus, trimmed and cut into 3/4 inch pieces.
- 1-pound lobster meat, thawed and 1/2-inch-diced
- ¼ cup parmesan
- ¼ cup almond milk

Directions
Heat broiler to low. In a mixing bowl, combine eggs, egg whites, milk, salt and pepper.

In a 12" ovenproof skillet over medium-high heat, heat oil. Cook onion, bell pepper and oregano, stirring occasionally until vegetables are somewhat soft, 3 minutes. Add diced asparagus, cook 3 minutes. Add lobster, cook until opaque, 3 minutes.

Pour egg mixture into the skillet, reduce heat to low. Cook, stirring occasionally, until egg begins to set but is set wet on top, 5 minutes. Cook, without stirring, 5 minutes. Transfer skillet to broiler, broil until golden, 5 minutes.

Remove from broiler, top and sprinkle with parmesan then slice into 4 wedges.

Homemade Chicken + Apple Sausage
Serves 6-8

These homemade breakfast sausages are so healthy and yummy, you won't believe it.

Ingredients
- 1 tablespoon extra virgin olive oil
- 1 small onion, peeled and quartered
- 2 apples cored and quartered
- 1-pound of boneless skinless chicken breast, 2 inch chunks
- ½ cup fresh basil leaves
- ¾ teaspoon fresh ground pepper
- ¾ teaspoon sea salt
- pinch of cinnamon

Directions
Place the onion, apples and basil into the blender and pulse until finely chopped.

Heat oil in medium skillet. Add the onion and apples, saute several minutes until soft. Remove from the skillet and place in a large bowl.

In the same blender, place the chicken then pulse until finely ground. Add the ground chicken to the bowl with the onion and apple mix. Add the cinnamon and season with salt and pepper. Mix well using your hands. Preheat the oven to 350 degrees. Form the mixture into 8 patties and bake on a greased cookie sheet for 10-12 minutes, or until fully cooked.

Serve over a bed of spinach, drizzle with oil olive.

Overnight Oats
Serves 1

A delicious ready to eat breakfast waiting for you!

Ingredients
- ½ cup gluten-free rolled oats
- ½ cup almond milk
- ½ cup fresh blueberries
- ½ teaspoon chia seeds
- pinch of salt
- pinch of cinnamon

Directions
Throw everything in a jar, screw the lid on top, shake, and off it goes into the fridge. The next morning add stevia (if you desired).

Gluten-Free Apple Cinnamon Pancakes
Serves 1

The easiest and healthiest pancakes you will ever make!

Ingredients
- 1 honeycrisp apple, cored and quartered
- ½ cup egg whites
- 1 teaspoon grass-fed butter
- ½ cup gluten-free rolled oats
- cinnamon
- stevia

Directions
Place apple, egg whites and oats into a blender and blend together.

Heat butter in skillet over medium heat. Pour oat mixture on the skillet to form small to medium sized pancakes. Cook each side 2 minutes or until golden.

Sprinkle cinnamon and stevia on top of cakes. Serve.

*Recipe inspired by my friend and fitness cover model, Lori Harder!

Almond Energy Pancakes
Serves 2-4

The best pancakes on the planet! Enjoy the texture and satisfying flavor of these super clean pancakes.

Ingredients
- 1 cup almond milk,
- 1 egg, beaten
- 3 tablespoons grass-fed butter
- 1 cup almond meal
- 1 ½ teaspoon baking soda
- ½ teaspoon sea salt.
- ¼ cup chia seeds
- ½ cup shredded coconut
- ½ cup walnuts
- 1 teaspoon stevia

Directions
Place the milk, egg, butter and stevia into the blender for 30 seconds. Add the almond meal, baking soda, salt, coconut and chia seeds and walnuts and blend additional 30 seconds. Allow batter to set for 20-30 minutes in the fridge.

Cook batter on medium heat until small bubbles form and edges are dry then flip. Cook until pancake center is puffed and springs back when gently pressed.

Top with fresh strawberries, cinnamon and stevia.

75

Fancy Oatmeal
Serves 1

A fancy twist on old-fashioned oatmeal.

Ingredients
- ½ cup old-fashioned rolled oats
- ½ teaspoon ground cinnamon
- ½ teaspoon stevia
- ½ cup pecans, chopped
- ½ cup blueberries (optional)
- 1 cup almond milk

Directions
Place the rolled oats, stevia and cinnamon in a microwave safe bowl. Pour in the almond milk, and stir to mix ingredients. Cook on high until water is absorbed, about 2 minutes. Stir in blueberries and pecans.

"Life has a way of teaching you your own strength. I had to learn that I am perfectly capable of taking care of myself and that I am a strong independent woman."

GREEN SMOOTHIES

The Good Start
Serves 1

Start your day off right with this power booster!

Ingredients
- 8-ounces of filtered water
- 1 teaspoon ginger root, peeled
- ½ cup ice
- 1 cup baby kale
- 1 honeycrisp apple, cored and quartered
- ½ cup broccoli
- 1 celery stalk, halved

Directions
Place all ingredients into a blender and blend.

Green Dream
Serves 1

A delicious way to drink your greens with a creamy consistency!

Ingredients
- 8-ounces of almond milk
- 1 tablespoon almond butter
- ½ cup ice
- 1 cup baby kale
- 1 green apple, cored and quartered
- ¼ cup fresh parsley

Directions
Place all ingredients into a blender and blend well.

Antioxidant Refresher
Serves 1

You won't taste the spinach in this refreshing antioxidant-rich smoothie.

Ingredients
- 8-ounces of coconut water
- 1 cup frozen blueberries
- 1 green apple, cored and quartered
- ½ cup cucumber, peeled and sliced
- ½ cup spinach

Directions
Place all ingredients into a blender and blend.

Green Goddess
Serves 1

My favorite green juice on the planet that fires up your metabolism, satisfies your belly and gives you a glow.

Ingredients
- 6-ounces of filtered water
- 1 teaspoon ginger root, peeled
- ½ cup ice
- 1 cup baby kale
- 1 honeycrisp or fuji apple, cored and quartered
- juice of 1 lemon
- cayenne pepper

Directions
Place all ingredients into a blender except cayenne, blend well then dust cayenne pepper on top.

PROTEIN POWER SHAKES

Protein shakes are great pre and post-workout meal options. It's best practice to drink a shake at least one hour before a workout for energy or within 30 minutes following your workout for muscle recovery.

Chocolate Supreme Protein Shake
Serves 1

My favorite post-workout recovery shake that tastes like a fudge brownie and helps with muscle soreness!

Ingredients
- 1 scoop chocolate protein powder
- 1 tablespoon almond butter
- ½ cup ice
- 1 teaspoon MCT or coconut oil
- 8-ounces of almond milk
- 1 teaspoon maca powder
- 1 teaspoon cacao powder

Directions
Place all ingredients into a blender, blend well and enjoy.

Spiced Frappuccino Protein Shake
Serves 1

A protein shake with a cafe latte twist and a coffee kick that will energize your day.

Ingredients
- 4-ounces of almond milk
- 4-ounces of brewed organic coffee
- ½ cup ice
- 1 scoop vanilla protein powder
- dash of cinnamon

Directions
Place all ingredients into a blender and blend well.

"Your highest well-being and true beauty is reflected in how often health and self-love influence your decisions."

Apple Almond Smoothie
Serves 1

A smoothie almost as good as apple pie but healthy for you and packed with protein!

Ingredients
- 1 scoop vanilla protein powder
- 1 tablespoon almond butter
- ½ cup ice
- 1 granny smith apple, peeled and cored
- 8-ounces of almond milk
- 1 teaspoon chia seeds
- pinch of cinnamon

Directions
Place all ingredients into a blender and blend.

Ginger Coconut Shake
Serves 1

A protein shake that will satisfy your hunger and helping you burn more fat.

Ingredients
- 8-ounces of coconut milk
- ½ cup shredded coconut
- 1 scoop of vanilla powder
- 1 teaspoon ginger root, peeled
- 1 teaspoon coconut or MCT oil
- ½ cup ice

Directions
Place all ingredients into a blender and blend well.

Blueberry Chocolate Antioxidant Shake
Serves 1

This smoothie will rock your world with flavor without the sugar overload!

Ingredients
- 1 scoop chocolate whey protein
- ¾ cup frozen blueberries
- ½ teaspoon vanilla extract
- 8-ounces of almond milk
- 1 square of at least 70% cacao dark chocolate
- pinch of pink sea salt

Directions
Place all ingredients into a blender, blend well and enjoy.

Berry Bliss Protein Shake
Serves 1

A protein shake packed with antioxidants!

Ingredients
- 1 cup frozen blueberries
- 4-ounces coconut milk
- 1 scoops vanilla whey protein powder
- 4-ounces water
- 1 teaspoon coconut oil
- 2 celery sticks, halved

Directions
Place all ingredients into a blender and blend.

Cinnamon Berry Shake
Serves 1

A very berry protein shake that is packed with vitamin C and antioxidants.

Ingredients
- ¼ cup frozen blueberries
- ½ cup frozen strawberries
- 1 scoop vanilla whey protein
- 1 teaspoon coconut or mct oil
- 8-ounces of coconut milk
- dash of cinnamon

Directions
Place all ingredients into a blender, blend and enjoy.

Peanut Butter Chocolate Protein Shake
Serves 1

A protein shake favorite that everybody loves.

Ingredients
- 1 tablespoon organic peanut butter
- 1 scoop chocolate whey protein
- ½ cup ice
- 8-ounces of almond milk

Directions
Place all ingredients into a blender, blend well and enjoy.

Mocha Freeze
Serves 1

If you love mocha frappuccinos then you will love this yummy protein shake

Ingredients
- 4-ounces of organic brewed coffee
- ½ cup ice
- 1 scoop chocolate whey protein
- 1 teaspoon coconut or MCT oil
- 4-ounces of almond milk

Directions
Place all ingredients into a blender and blend.

LUNCH
POWER SALADS

Ground Turkey BLT Salad
Serves 4-6

If you love ground turkey then you will love this easy and yummy salad.

Ingredients
- 4 slices bacon, diced
- 1-pound ground turkey burger
- 4 cups romaine lettuce, chopped
- 1 avocado, diced
- 1 cup cherry tomatoes, halved
- ¼ cup crumbled feta cheese

Directions
Heat a large skillet over medium high heat. Add bacon and cook until brown and crispy, about 6-8 minutes. Add the ground turkey to the skillet, season with salt and pepper then cook through until brown.

In a large bowl combine romaine lettuce, avocado, tomato, feta cheese, cooked ground turkey and bacon. Drizzle with *Balsamic Vinaigrette Dressing*, see page 108 for recipe. Serve.

Tuscan Kale Salad
Serves 2-4

A gorgeous salad that is cleansing and satisfying at the same time!

Ingredients
- 1 bunch tuscan kale (also known as black or lacinato kale)
- ½ cup raw sliced almonds
- ¼ cup finely grated parmesan
- 3 tablespoons extra virgin olive oil
- freshly squeezed juice of 1 lemon
- ¼ teaspoon salt
- Freshly ground black pepper to taste

Directions
Remove stems and ribs from kale and discard. Slice kale into 3/4-inch-wide ribbons. You should have 4 to 5 cups. Place kale in a large bowl.

Squeeze lemon juice over kale and give kale a nice massage. Then add the oil and massage again really breaking down the kale structure.

Place bowl in fridge for at least 30 minutes to soften the kale. Remove from fridge top with almonds, parmesan and a drizzle of oil. Serve

Grilled Salmon Arugula Salad
Serves 1

A beautiful healthy salad that is light and refreshing, great for summertime!

Ingredients
- 1 wild salmon fillet
- bag of organic arugula
- ¼ cup crumbled goat cheese
- 2 cara cara oranges - peeled and thinly sliced
- 2 tablespoon extra virgin olive oil
- salt and pepper
- squeeze lemon
- avocado, ripe and cubed

Directions
Turn on grill to low medium heat and let warm up for 5 minutes. Rub both sides of salmon fillet in oil. Place salmon on grill and cook until flaky, 3 to 5 minutes on each side.

Combine arugula, goat cheese, orange slices, lemon juice, 1 tablespoon of oil, avocado, salt and pepper to taste in a large bowl. Mix all ingredients. Place salad mixture on a plate.

Remove salmon from grill and serve over salad mixture and drizzle with remaining olive oil. Enjoy.

Spicy Shrimp Salad
Serves 2-4

This salad will spice up your metabolism and afternoon!

Ingredients
- 1 pound peeled and deveined large shrimp
- 1 tablespoon coconut oil
- 1 avocado diced
- ¼ cup celery, chopped
- 1 garlic clove, minced
- ¼ onion, chopped
- ¼ teaspoon chili powder
- ½ teaspoon cumin
- 10 sprigs of cilantro with stems, minced
- salt to taste
- 2 teaspoons fresh lime juice
- 3 cups romaine

Directions
Heat a grill pan over medium-high heat. Sprinkle shrimp with salt and black pepper. Coat pan with coconut oil. Add shrimp to pan; cook 2 minutes on each side or until done. Remove shrimp from pan and cool for 5 minutes.

Place shrimp in a medium bowl; stir in the remaining ingredients except romaine. Arrange lettuce on plates; top with shrimp mixture.

Zucchini Noodles

How to make fresh zucchini noodles instead of inflammatory pastas!

Ingredients
- 2 medium-sized raw zucchini squash, washed, dried, and trimmed at both ends
- 2 tablespoon fresh-squeezed lemon juice
- salt and pepper to taste
- herbs of your choice

Directions
Using the julienne blade of a mandoline, spiralizer vegetable slicer or slice zucchini into long, thin strands. Slice the zucchini just until you reach the seeds in the middle and then stop (the seeds will cause the noodles to fall apart). NOTE: If you don't have a mandoline or a spiral slicer, you can either use a vegetable peeler or a knife.

Separate the zucchini strands. Transfer zucchini strands to a colander set over a mixing bowl. Toss the zucchini strands with salt; let stand 15 minutes at room temperature.

After 15 minutes, gently squeeze the zucchini strands to extract any excess water. Transfer drained zucchini strands to a bowl and toss with lemon juice, salt and pepper.

Garnish with herbs of your choice.

Serving Ideas:
- Top with marinara or pesto sauce
- Use in place of pasta
- Top with peanut sauce

Raw Zucchini Noodle Salad

Serves 2-4

A new gluten-free twist on pasta salad and just as good in taste!

Ingredients
- ¼ cup extra virgin olive oil
- 2 tablespoons lemon juice
- 1 can olives, sliced and drained
- 1-2 cloves garlic, minced
- ¼ cup chopped fresh basil
- salt and pepper
- 2 medium zucchini, cut in half and stems removed
- 1 cup halved cherry tomatoes
- 1 medium cucumber, chopped
- ½ cup shredded parmesan cheese

Directions
Combine oil, lemon juice, garlic and basil together in a food processor and process just until emulsified. Season to taste with salt and pepper. Set aside.

Using the 1/8 inch spacing blade or spiralizer, cut the zucchini into noodles.

Place zucchini, cucumber, tomatoes, olive oil olive mixture and parmesan together in a bowl. Cover and refrigerate for 20 minutes. Serve.

Thai Chicken Salad
Serves 2-4

This is a sweet and delightful salad with tons of flavor and protein.

Ingredients
- 1 bag romaine
- ¼ cup red onions, chopped
- ½ cup mandarin oranges
- ½ cup almonds, sliced
- 10 sprigs of cilantro with stems, minced
- 1 cup *Simple Shredded Chicken*, recipe opposite page
- 1-2 tablespoons *Sesame Dressing*, recipe below

Directions
Combine all ingredients in a large mixing bowl then serve.

Sesame Dressing
Serves 1

A naturally sweet dressing without any added or refined sugar.

Ingredients
- ¼ teaspoon stevia
- juice from 1 lemon
- 1 tablespoon sesame oil
- 1 teaspoon sesame seeds

Directions
Combine all ingredients and mix together.

Simple Shredded Chicken
Serves 3-4

You won't believe how fast and easy this shredded chicken is, great for preparing a quick lunch or dinner.

Ingredients
- 1 tablespoon olive oil
- 4 boneless, skinless chicken breasts
- salt and pepper
- ¾ cup water

Directions
In a large 12-inch nonstick skillet with a lid, heat the olive oil over medium heat until hot and rippling. Season the chicken with salt and pepper on both sides.

Place the chicken top-side down in the hot skillet and let the chicken cook for 5 minutes until golden brown on top. Flip the chicken, add the water or chicken broth, cover the skillet and let the chicken simmer gently over medium heat for 7-10 minutes until the chicken is cooked through. Don't overcook or it might be dry.

While the chicken is simmering, add additional water ¼ cup at a time if the liquid evaporates too quickly. Remove the chicken from the skillet. Let it cool slightly before shredding. The cooked chicken will keep well-covered in the refrigerator for up to 3 days or can be frozen for up to 2 months.

Healthy Shredded Chicken Taco Salad
Serves 4-6

If you love Mexican food then this salad is for you.

Ingredients
- 2 cups *Simple Shredded Chicken*, cooked, recipe page 103
- 2 tablespoons taco seasoning
- ¼ cup olive oil
- 2 tablespoons butter
- 1 head of lettuce, shredded thin
- 3 tomatoes, diced
- ½ cup feta cheese
- 2 avocados, diced
- 3 green onions, sliced
- ½ cup fresh cilantro leaves, chopped
- ¼ cup salsa

Directions
For the chicken, generously sprinkle with the taco seasoning. Heat the oil and butter in a large skillet over medium-high heat. Warm up chicken until fully seasoned, about 2 minutes. Set aside to cool.

On a platter, layer the shredded lettuce, shredded chicken, tomatoes, cheese, avocados, green onions and cilantro. Top with salsa. Serve the salad in individual bowls.

Chicken Avocado Salad
Serves 2-4

A healthy and refreshing way to do chicken salad.

Ingredients
- 2 cups *Simple Shredded Chicken*, cooked, recipe page 103
- 1 avocado, diced
- 1 celery stalk, chopped
- ¼ sweet onion, chopped
- ½ lime, juiced
- ¼ cup tomato, diced
- 1 tablespoon extra virgin olive oil
- 2 tablespoons fresh cilantro, chopped
- pinch cayenne pepper (optional)
- salt and ground black pepper to taste

Directions
In a large bowl combine all ingredients and serve.

Great served over with quinoa.

Grilled Vegetable Salad
Serves 2-4

This salad is a veggie lover's dream.

Ingredients
- 2 cups romaine, chopped
- 1 avocado, cut into bite-size chunks
- 1 ripe tomato cut into bite-size chunks
- *Grilled Balsamic Vegetables,* recipe page 159
- *Dijon Mustard Dressing,* recipe below

Directions
Combine romaine, avocado and tomato in a bowl and top with grilled balsamic vegetables and drizzle with dijon mustard dressing. Serve.

Dijon Mustard Dressing
Serves 2-4

A light tangy dressing that satisfies and elevates any salad.

Ingredients
- 1 teaspoon dijon mustard
- 1 teaspoon fresh lemon juice
- 1 teaspoon fresh lime juice
- ½ teaspoon white wine vinegar
- ½ cup extra virgin olive oil
- salt and pepper to taste

Directions
Combine all ingredients in a bowl, whisk until smooth then season with salt and pepper. Serve.

Superwoman Salad
Serves 2-4

This salad will refuel and re-energize your day to keep you going strong!

Ingredients
- 2 cups baby spinach
- 1 cup mushrooms, chopped
- 1 cup broccoli, chopped
- 1 tomato, chopped
- 1 avocado, diced
- 2 tablespoons extra virgin oil olive
- ¼ teaspoon sea salt
- ¼ teaspoon black pepper
- 1 lemon

Directions
Combine all fresh ingredients in a bowl. For dressing, drizzle olive oil and fresh squeezed lemon juice over salad, add sea salt and pepper to taste.

Arugula Salad
Serves 4-6

A delightful salad that keeps your hunger in check.

Ingredients
- 1 bag of Arugula Salad
- 2 tablespoons of extra virgin olive oil
- ½ cup sliced almonds
- ½ cup cherry tomatoes
- ¼ cup parmesan cheese

Directions
Combine all ingredients in large salad bowl and serve.

Chopped Chicken Lettuce Wraps
Serves 1

You won't believe how fast this salad comes together, great for an on-the-go lunch.

Ingredients
- 1 cup romaine lettuce, large chunks
- 4-ounces of cooked chicken breast
- ½ cup cherry tomatoes
- ¼ cup kalamata olives, pitted
- ½ cup feta cheese

Directions
Place all of the ingredients in a blender except lettuce and pulse for 3 pulses or until the desired chop is achieved. Serve over lettuce cups and drizzle with *Balsamic Vinaigrette Dressing*, recipe below.

Balsamic Vinaigrette Dressing
Serves 2-4

A homemade go-to healthy and yummy dressing.

Ingredients
- ¼ cup extra virgin olive oil
- 2 tablespoons balsamic vinegar
- ½ tablespoon red wine vinegar
- 1 clove garlic, minced
- ¼ teaspoon ground mustard
- 1 tablespoon lemon juice

Directions
Whisk all the ingredients together. That's it!

Broccoli Feta Salad
Serves 1-2

Get your nutrients with this yummy way to do broccoli.

Ingredients
- 2 cups steamed broccoli
- ½ cup feta cheese
- 1 tablespoon *Champagne Vinaigrette*, recipe below

Directions
Combine all ingredients together and serve.

Champagne Vinaigrette Dressing
Serves 4-6

A light and refreshing dressing option.

Ingredients
- 2 teaspoons dijon mustard
- ¼ cup champagne vinegar
- ¾ cup extra-virgin olive oil
- ½ teaspoon salt
- pinch of freshly ground black pepper

Directions
In a small bowl, combine mustard and vinegar; whisk together. While whisking constantly, slowly drizzle in olive oil. Season with salt and pepper.

Grilled Romaine Salad
Serves 2-4

A new and healthy way to do salad.

Ingredients
- 3 to 4 romaine hearts
- 3 tablespoons olive oil
- 1 tablespoons red wine vinegar
- 2 teaspoons chopped fresh herbs such as rosemary, thyme, oregano (or 1 teaspoon dried mixed herbs)
- ¼ teaspoon salt
- pinch freshly ground black pepper

Directions
Prep the romaine hearts—pull off any old leaves. Chop off the top 1 or 2 inches of the lettuce head, and shave off the browned part of the root end, leaving the root end intact so that the lettuce head stays together.

Prepare your grill for high, direct heat. Paint the lettuce hearts all over with the vinaigrette. Prepare the vinaigrette. Put the oil, vinegar, herbs, salt and pepper in a small bowl and whisk with a fork to combine.

Grill the romaine hearts until lightly browned on all sides, turning every minute or two until done. Serve immediately. You can either serve the hearts whole, or chop them and toss them for a salad.

SOULFUL SOUPS

Dream of Broccoli Soup
Serves 2-4

This vegan soup is super filling and a great way to get your greens.

Ingredients
- ¼ cup raw cashews, soaked overnight
- ½ cup small onion, chopped
- 1 clove garlic, chopped
- 1 tablespoon extra virgin olive oil
- 1 ½ cups broccoli
- ½ teaspoon garlic powder

Directions
Place all of the ingredients into a saucepan and bring to a boil. Reduce heat and simmer 20 minutes, until broccoli and onions are tender. Remove from the heat and allow to cool.

Place the cooled ingredients into the blender and puree. Return the soup to the saucepan and simmer until heated through. Add salt and pepper to taste.

Butternut Squash Soup
Serves 4

This dairy-free soup is super creamy from the cashews and hits the spot!

Ingredients
- 3 tablespoons extra virgin olive oil
- 1 yellow onion, chopped
- 1 cup raw cashews
- 1 large apple, cored and chopped
- 1 large carrot, peeled and chopped
- 2-pounds of butternut squash, cubed
- 1 teaspoon fresh thyme
- 4 cups of vegetable stock
- ½ teaspoon sea salt
- black pepper to taste

Directions
Heat oil in a large saucepan and add the onions, cooking until they begin to soften about 5 mins. Add the cashews and cook, stirring for about 5 mins.

Add the carrot, apple, squash and thyme to the pot and cook for 5 minutes. Add the stock and stir to combine. Bring the soup to a boil and reduce the heat to med-low, allowing to simmer until the squash is easily pierced with a knife. 20 to 25 minutes. Remove from the heat.

Allow the soup to cool to room temperature. Working in batches, ladle the soup into a blender. Secure the lid and puree. Heat soup to desired temperature before serving and dust with cinnamon.

Turkey, Kale & Brown Rice Soup
Serves 4-6

This hearty soup comforts on a cold day, is packed full of flavor and nutrition!

Ingredients
- 2 tablespoons extra-virgin olive oil
- 5 to 6 large shallots, chopped
- 1 1/2, white mushrooms cut into 1/2-inch pieces
- 1 large red bell pepper, cut into 1/2-inch pieces (about 1 1/2 cups)
- 8-ounces ground white turkey meat, broken into small chunks
- 1 tablespoon herbs: basil, rosemary, thyme and garlic
- 4 cups low-sodium chicken broth, plus more as needed
- 15-ounce can diced tomatoes in juice, drained
- 1 cup cooked brown rice
- 1 small bunch kale, coarsely chopped (about 4 packed cups)
- 1 teaspoon sea salt
- ½ teaspoon freshly ground black pepper
- ¼ cup chopped fresh flat-leaf parsley
- ¼ cup freshly grated parmesan

Directions
Heat the oil in a large pot over medium-high heat. Add the shallots, mushrooms and bell pepper and saute, stirring frequently, until the vegetables begin to brown and soften slightly, 8 to 10 minutes.

Add the ground turkey and stir until the meat turns white and begins to color very slightly around the edges, 5 to 7 minutes. Add the herbs and stir, 1 minute. Add 4 cups broth, tomatoes and rice. Bring to a boil. Stir in the kale and season with salt and the freshly ground black pepper.

Reduce the heat to medium-low. Cover and simmer until the vegetables are tender, about 15 minutes. Ladle the soup into bowls.

Sprinkle each serving with parsley and parmesan and serve.

BUNLESS BURGERS

Bunless Bacon & Avocado Burgers
Serves 6

The best gluten-free recipe for a homemade hamburger.

Ingredients
- 6 pieces crispy bacon
- 2-pounds ground organic grass-fed beef
- 3 avocados, pitted and sliced
- 1 teaspoon garlic powder
- 1 head iceberg lettuce
- 2 teaspoon onion powder
- ½ cup egg whites
- 2 large ripe tomatoes, sliced
- 1 teaspoon worcestershire
- 1 teaspoon black pepper, fresh ground
- ½ teaspoon sea salt
- ½ cup gluten-free rolled oats
- 1 tablespoon extra virgin olive oil
- ½ cup feta cheese
- 1 lemon

Directions
Combine turkey, garlic powder, onion powder, egg whites, worcestershire, pepper, salt and oats in a large mixing bowl. Separate into 6 burger patties.

Heat grill to low to medium heat. Cook burgers until done to your liking.

Place burger on top of a piece of iceberg lettuce then top burger with crispy bacon, feta, a tomato slice, some avocado slices, a second piece of iceberg lettuce and drizzle with the lemon juice. Top with plenty of fresh ground pepper and enjoy with a knife and fork.

Lettuce Wrapped Bison Burgers
Serves 4-6

A bold and lean way to-do a burger without feeling guilty, enjoy it!

Ingredients
- 1 1/2 pounds lean ground buffalo
- 1 medium onion, finely chopped, about 1 cup
- 1 tablespoon paprika
- 2 teaspoons dijon mustard
- 1 teaspoon minced garlic
- 3/4 teaspoon freshly ground pepper
- 1/4 teaspoon salt
- 1/4 teaspoon liquid smoke
- salt and pepper to taste
- 1 head of iceberg lettuce
- ½ cup pico de gallo
- 1 avocado, sliced
- 2 tablespoons olive oil
- 4 mild green chiles
- large romaine lettuce chunks

Directions
Preheat an outdoor grill to medium-high. Put the buffalo, onion, garlic, mustard, paprika, and liquid smoke in a large bowl and season generously with salt and pepper. Mix everything together with your hands until it is well combined.

Take about 1 cup (8 ounces) of the meat mixture and form it into patties with your hands. When you have them all made, grill them, turning frequently, until cooked through, about 8 to 10 minutes total. (Alternately, cook them in a large nonstick skillet over medium-high heat until cooked through, about 8 to 10 minutes.)

In a large heavy skillet, heat oil over medium-high. When oil is very hot, add chiles. Cook, turning occasionally, until browned and blistered on all sides, about 10 minutes. Season with salt, Slice them open, lengthwise, and scrape out the seeds with a knife or spoon.

Top burgers with sliced and sauted green chiles, avocado and pico de gallo then wrap in lettuce.

Bunless Salmon Burgers
Serves 4-6

A delicious and different way to enjoy salmon!

Ingredients
- ½ teaspoon extra virgin olive oil
- 1 garlic clove
- 1 ½-pounds skinless wild salmon fillets, cut into 2-inch chunks
- 1 small red onion, chopped
- 1 red bell pepper, chopped and seeded
- ¼ cup fresh parsley leaves
- salt and pepper to taste
- spinach, tomato slices and healthy tarter sauce (for serving)

Directions
Preheat the broiler with rack 4 inches from the heat source. Grease a rimmed baking sheet with the oil.

Combine the garlic and 1/3 of salmon in a food processor. Process to a puree, stopping to scrape down the sides as necessary.

Add the remaining salmon along with the onion, bell pepper, parsley, and salt and pepper to taste. Pulse until the salmon is chopped but not too finely. Shape the mixture into 4 patties and put on the prepared baking sheet.

Broil until the side exposed to the heat develops a browned crust (3-5 minutes). Carefully turning the burgers and repeat on other side, cooking until the salmon has turned opaque throughout. Serve on top of spinach topped with healthy tarter sauce spread and tomato.

Healthy Tarter Sauce
Serves 2-4

A no mayonnaise tartar sauce that's healthy for you!

Ingredients
- 1 ripe avocado
- 2 teaspoon grass-fed butter
- ½ tablespoon chopped dill pickles
- 1 tsp garlic powder
- squeeze of lemon juice

Directions
Combine all ingredients in a food processor and mix well. Refrigerate until you serve. Should last for a few days in a sealed container in the fridge.

HEALTHY SNACKS

Kale & Artichoke Dip with Cucumber
Serves 2 ½ cups

A super yummy way to eat kale and have a healthy snack!

Ingredients
- 1 ripe avocado
- ¼ cup grass-fed butter
- 4-ounces of almond milk
- 2 tablespoons lemon juice
- 1 teaspoon of extra virgin olive oil
- 14-ounce can of artichoke hearts, drained and chopped
- ½ cup parmesan cheese
- 2 tablespoons chopped onions
- 1 cup frozen kale, thawed, excess liquid removed

Directions
Preheat oven to 350 degrees F. Place all of the ingredients into a blender except cucumber and pulse until ingredients are combined. Spoon the dip into a baking dish and bake for 20 mins. Serve with sliced cucumbers season with salt and pepper.

Oatmeal Fiber Bars
Serves 6-8

Delicious gluten-free oatmeal bars, a great sweet tooth substitution or healthy snack!

Ingredients
- 2 cups unsweetened almond milk
- 2 cups gluten-free rolled oats
- ½ cup pecans
- ½ cup dark chocolate at least 70% cacao, chopped
- ½ cup ground flax seeds (not whole flax seeds)
- 2 teaspoons pure vanilla extract
- 1 ½ teaspoon ground cinnamon
- 4 cups pink lady apples, cored and grated
- ½ cup blueberries

Directions
Preheat oven to 350°F.

Combine apple, blueberries, pecans and milk in blender and mix well. Then mix all ingredients together in a large bowl. If mixture isn't thick enough, add more oats.

Transfer to a parchment-paper-lined 9-inch square baking pan, press down and smooth out the top and bake until firm and golden brown, about 1 hour. Let cool in the pan; cut into squares and serve warm or at room temperature.

Spicy Cauliflower Bites
Serves 2-4

A spicy snack that revs up the metabolism.

Ingredients
- 1 large head of cauliflower, cleaned and cut into pieces
- 3 tablespoons olive oil
- 1 ½ teaspoon cayenne pepper
- 2 cups almond meal
- 1 teaspoon sea salt
- 1 teaspoon cumin
- hot sauce

Directions
Preheat oven to 425 degrees F. Line a baking sheet with aluminum foil or parchment paper.
In a small bowl mix the almond meal, salt, cumin and cayenne.

In another large bowl toss the cauliflower with the olive oil so that each piece is covered. Roll the cauliflower pieces in the almond meal mixture and make sure each piece is coated with the spice mixture. Drizzle top with hot sauce.

Place the cauliflower on the baking sheet and bake for 30 to 45 minutes or until golden brown. You will have to turn it every 15 minutes or so to make sure it browns on all sides.

Kale Chips
Serves 4-6 cups

A crunchy salty snack that is surprisingly tasty!

Ingredients
- 1 bag baby kale
- 2 tablespoons extra virgin olive oil
- 1 teaspoon garlic powder
- salt and pepper to taste

Directions
Combine kale with oil, sprinkle with pepper, pink himalayan salt and garlic powder in a large bowl. Bake at 400 degrees F for 20 minutes.

Nut Mix
Serves 15 cups

Try my awesome nut mix recipe!

Ingredients
- 1 pound raw shelled walnuts
- 1 pound raw shelled pistachios
- 1 pound dry roasted almonds
- 1 pound dry roasted peanuts
- 1 pound raw pepitas

Directions
Mix all ingredients in a large mixing bowl, portion out 1/4 servings into individual plastic bags. Then place individual portions in the refrigerator or freezer. Add pink sea salt to taste.

Sauteed Almonds
Serves 2 cups

A fancy way to eat nuts and great crowd pleaser!

Ingredients
- ½ cup olive oil
- ½-pound raw almonds
- ½ teaspoon sea salt
- ¼ tsp garlic powder
- 1 tablespoon black pepper
- ¼ teaspoon cayenne pepper
- 1 teaspoon dried oregano
- 1 teaspoon dried thyme

Directions
In a large frying pan, heat the oil over medium-high heat for 2 minutes or until an almond dropped into the oil sizzles. Add almonds to the pan, lower the heat, and saute, stirring often, until the color of light caramel, about 5 minutes. Remove with a slotted spoon and drain on paper towels. Repeat with remaining almonds.

Place in a medium bowl and toss to coat with all seasonings. Serve warm or let cool and keep in an airtight container for up to 1 week.

Peanut Butter Sushi Bites
Serves 1-2

Peanut butter always satisfies any sweet craving!

Ingredients
- 1 gluten-free tortilla wrap
- 1 tablespoon organic peanut butter, thinly sliced
- 1 honeycrisp apple
- dash of cinnamon and stevia

Directions
Spread peanut butter over the entire face of the wrap. Thinly slice the apple and set it on top of the wrap toward the front or back sprinkle with cinnamon and stevia, forming one long sushi roll.

Slice into bite-size pieces and enjoy.

"It's ok to NOT be perfect 100% of the time on your diet because at any moment you can choose to be healthy again."

DIVINE DINNERS

Brussel Sprouts+Bacon+Cauliflower Casserole
Serves 6-8

This flavorful dish is great for the family and the waistline!

Ingredients
- 1-pounds brussels sprouts, cleaned and trimmed
- 1 cup grated parmesan
- 1 teaspoon fresh thyme leaves
- salt and black pepper
- 2 cups almond milk
- 1 tablespoons extra-virgin olive oil
- 1 cup bacon, cooked and chopped
- 1 teaspoon fresh parsley, chopped
- 2 cups *Cauliflower Couscous*, recipe page 155

Directions
Preheat the oven to 350 degrees F.

Shave the brussels sprouts horizontally into 1/8-inch slices with a sharp knife or mandoline. Add to a bowl. Add couscous, cooked and chopped bacon bits and thyme to the bowl. Toss to combine. Add the mixture to a baking dish, packing it in. Pour over the almond milk.

In a small bowl combine parmesan and olive oil then pour over the brussels sprouts mixture.

Bake uncovered until the brussels sprouts are tender, the sauce is bubbling and the top is golden, 25 to 30 minutes. Garnish with the parsley and serve.

FREE RANGE CHICKEN & TURKEY

Baked Chicken Breast with Mushroom & Spinach Saute
Serves 2-4

Make chicken more exciting with this healthy recipe!

Ingredients
- 4 boneless skinless chicken breast halves
- 1 tablespoon olive oil
- 1 pinch garlic powder
- salt and pepper to taste
- 1 cup mushrooms
- 1 cup spinach
- 1 teaspoon extra virgin olive oil

Directions
Preheat oven to 350 degrees F. Rub each chicken breast with olive oil, then place in a lightly greased 9x13 inch baking dish using coconut oil cooking spray. Season with garlic powder, salt and pepper to taste. Cover dish with aluminum foil and bake in the preheated oven for 45 minutes. Check chicken and remove cover if desired. Bake for another 15 minutes.

In saute pan, add 1 teaspoon olive oil. Saute mushrooms for 2 to 3 minutes. Add in spinach and garlic. Cook for 3 more minutes. Squeeze half of a fresh lemon over the top. Season with sea salt and pepper to taste.

Jerk Chicken with Avocado Compound Butter
Serves 2-4

Don't be a jerk to yourself, love your body with this super delicious recipe!

Ingredients
- ¾ teaspoon salt
- 1 teaspoon ground allspice
- 1 teaspoon ground cumin
- ¼ teaspoon dried thyme
- ¼ teaspoon cayenne pepper
- ¼ teaspoon cinnamon
- 4 boneless skinless chicken breasts
- 1 teaspoon grass-fed butter
- 2 teaspoons *Avocado Compound Butter*, recipe page 151

Directions
In a bowl combine, salt, allspice, cumin, thyme, cayenne and cinnamon, rub over both sides of chicken breasts.

In a large skillet over medium heat, heat grass-fed butter; cook chicken breasts until cooked through, 10-12 minutes each side.

Remove from skillet, top with cilantro lime butter and let cool for 5 minutes. Serve with avocado compound butter.

Healthy Baked 'Fried' Chicken
Serves 4-6

A classic southern comfort food made healthy!

Ingredients
- 6 boneless skinless chicken breasts
- 3 cups almond meal flour
- sea salt and freshly ground pepper
- ½ cup organic almond milk
- 2 tablespoons Grass-fed Butter
- 2 tablespoons dijon mustard
- ¼ teaspoon cayenne pepper
- 1 ½ teaspoons paprika
- ½ teaspoon ground cumin
- 3 cups spinach

Directions
Preheat the oven to 425 degrees F.

Rinse the chicken in cold water; pat dry. In a wide bowl or on a plate, season the almond meal flour with salt and 1/4 teaspoon pepper. Dredge each chicken piece through the flour so it's fully coated, tap against the bowl to shake off excess flour and set aside. Discard the flour.

In a blender, mix the milk, mustard, cayenne pepper, paprika, butter and sage. Give each floured chicken piece a good milk bath and then roll it again through the almond meal.

Arrange the chicken pieces on baking sheet and place in the hot oven.
Cook for 15 to 20 minutes, lower the heat to 375 degrees and cook for another 25 to 30 minutes, until cooked through. The juices should run clear when the meat is pierced with a knife. Serve over spinach.

Quinoa Stir-fry with Chicken & Veggies
Serves 4-6

A perfect and healthy family dinner!

Ingredients
- ¾ cup quinoa, rinsed
- ½ teaspoon salt
- 1 tablespoon MCT oil
- 1 red bell pepper, chopped
- ½ cup mushrooms, sliced
- 2 teaspoons fresh ginger, chopped
- 1 garlic clove, sliced
- 2 cups snow peas trimmed
- ½ cup raw cashews
- ¼ teaspoon black pepper
- 1 egg, beaten
- 6-ounces grilled chicken breast, chopped
- 2 scallions, chopped
- ½ cup fresh cilantro, chopped
- 1 teaspoon braggs amino acids

Directions
Place quinoa in a small sauce pan with ¾ cup water and ¼ teaspoon sea salt. Bring to a boil, then reduce heat to low. Cover and cook, undisturbed, until quinoa absorbs water, 15 minutes. remove from the heat, fluff with fork, and leave uncovered.

In a large skillet over medium to high heat, heat oil. Cook mushrooms, stirring occasionally, 1 minute. Add bell pepper, ginger and garlic, cook for 2 minutes. Add peas, spring with the remaining salt and pepper and cook 1 minute.

Remove veggies and return skillet to heat, add quinoa, along with the egg. Cook and stir until egg is evenly distributed, 2 minutes. Add vegetables, chicken, scallions, cilantro and soy sauce, and cashews cook 5 minutes. Serve warm.

Parmesan Crusted Chicken
Serves 4

A quick dinner recipe and kid favorite!

Ingredients
- ¼ cup parmesan cheese, grated
- 2 tablespoons of almond meal
- ¼ teaspoon paprika
- ¼ cup almond meal
- ½ teaspoon garlic powder
- ¼ teaspoon fresh ground pepper
- 4 boneless skinless chicken breast

Directions
Preheat oven to 400 degrees F.

In resealable plastic bag, combine cheese and all seasonings; shake well. Transfer mixture to plate; dip each chicken breast in cheese mixture, turning to coat all sides.

Place in a lightly greased baking dish. Bake for 45 minutes. Check chicken and remove if cooked through.

Healthier Than Mom's Meatloaf
Serves 4-6

The most delicious and healthy meatloaf you will ever taste!

Ingredients
- 1 yellow onion, quartered
- 4 cloves garlic
- ½ cup mushrooms, sliced
- 1 celery stalk, quartered
- 2 ½ cup baby kale
- 1 tablespoon chia seeds, soaked in 1/4 cup water for 15 minutes
- 1 ½-pound ground lean turkey
- 1 ¼ cup quinoa, cooked and cooled
- 3 tablespoons braggs amino acids
- ½ teaspoon ground black pepper
- ¼ cup no-sugar-added ketchup

Directions
Preheat the oven to 425°F. Line a small baking sheet with parchment paper.

Combine onion and garlic in a food processor and pulse until finely chopped. Transfer to a large skillet. Combine mushrooms and celery in the processor and pulse until chopped. Add kale and pulse a few times more. Add to the skillet.

Set the skillet over medium heat and cook, stirring, until vegetables release their liquid. Continue cooking, stirring frequently, until liquid evaporates and vegetables begin to brown, about 8 minutes; add water 1 tablespoon at a time if needed to prevent vegetables from sticking. Transfer to a large bowl and let cool slightly.

Add chia seeds, ground meat, quinoa, soy sauce and pepper to the bowl and mix gently with your hands. Scrape mixture onto the prepared baking sheet and form into a loaf about 4 inches wide and 10 inches long; dampen your hands if the mixture is very sticky. Spread top of loaf with ketchup.

Bake until cooked through and browned, about 40 minutes. Let cool for 5 minutes before slicing.

Pistachio Pesto Sauce
Serves 2

A delicious and satisfying way to do pesto sauce!

Ingredients
- ½ cup pistachios shells removed
- ½ cup basil leaves
- 1 large garlic clove
- 2 tablespoons parmesan
- ½ juice of a lemon
- salt and pepper to taste
- ½ cup extra virgin olive oil or more as needed

Directions
Add the pistachios, basil, garlic, parmesan, lemon juice, oil, salt and pepper to a blender and blend until desired consistency is achieved.

*Serve over steak, chicken, turkey or pasta.

Turkey Pesto Meatballs
Serves 25-30 meatballs

Serve these bite-sized treats to your friends as an appetizer or to your family as a quick and delicious meal.

Ingredients
- 2-pounds ground turkey
- ½ cup almond flour
- ½ cup *Pistachio Pesto Sauce*, recipe opposite page
- 2 egg whites
- ½ teaspoon salt
- ¼ teaspoon freshly ground pepper

Directions
Preheat the oven to 375 degrees F.

Line a baking sheet with aluminum foil and then place a wire cooling rack on top of the baking sheet. Coat the wire rack well with coconut oil or grass-fed butter.

In a large bowl, mix together all of the ingredients. Roll the mixture into small balls using your hands and place on the wire rack. Bake for 20-25 minutes until cooked through and browned on all sides.

*Serve over zucchini noodles and drizzle with extra virgin olive oil or marinara sauce.

FISH

Macadamia & Parmesan Crusted Tilapia
Serves 4

A rich, full flavor entree, this dinner recipe will have your family wanting seconds!

Ingredients
- ¾ cup macadamia nuts
- ¼ cup parmesan cheese
- ¼ cup almond meal
- ¼ teaspoon sea salt
- ¼ teaspoon pepper
- 4 tablespoons coconut cream from a can of coconut milk
- 4 tilapia fillets

Directions
Preheat oven to 350 degrees F.

Place the macadamia nuts and parmesan into the blender and blend until desired chop. Transfer chopped nuts to a mixing bowl, then add the almond meal, salt and pepper stirring to combine.

Spoon 1 teaspoon on each tilapia fillet with the coconut cream. Spread the crust mixture evenly on the top. Lightly coat a baking pan with cooking spray and arrange fish on the pan.

Bake for 20 minutes or until fish is cooked through.

Almond Crusted Salmon With Sauted Spinach
Serves 4

A delicious and healthy meal for a family dinner or date night!

Ingredients
- ¼ cup almond meal
- ¼ teaspoon ground coriander
- ⅛ teaspoon ground cumin
- 4 (6-ounce) salmon fillets, about 1-inch thick
- 2 teaspoon lemon juice
- ½ teaspoon sea salt
- ¼ teaspoon freshly ground black pepper
- ½ cup spinach
- ½ cup mushroom, sliced
- ½ teaspoon olive oil
- 1 teaspoon garlic

Directions
Preheat oven to 500° F.

Combine first 3 ingredients in a shallow dish; set aside.

Brush tops and sides of fish with juice: sprinkle with salt and pepper. Dredge top and sides in almond mixture; place skin side down on broiler pan coated with cooking spray. Sprinkle any remaining crumb mixture evenly over fish; press gently to adhere.

Bake for 15 minutes or until fish flakes easily when tested with a fork or until desired degree of doneness.

In saute pan, add 1 tsp olive oil. Saute the mushrooms for 2 minutes. Add in spinach and garlic. Cook for 3 more minutes. Add salt and pepper to taste. Serve salmon over sauteed spinach.

Salmon with Lemon, Asparagus and Rosemary
Serves 2

A lovely and healthy dinner for 2 that keeps you satisfied!

Ingredients
- 2 salmon fillets
- 1 lemon
- 1 bundle asparagus, washed and trimmed
- sea salt and pepper
- 1 teaspoon garlic powder
- 4 rosemary sprigs
- 2 tablespoons of extra virgin olive oil

Directions
Preheat oven to 500 degrees F.

Place salmon fillets into a baking sheet and line asparagus around the fillets. Sprinkle salmon and asparagus with the garlic powder then season with salt and pepper, drizzle oil over the top and place the rosemary sprigs on top of filets.

Bake for 15-20 minutes until salmon is flakey and opaque. Enjoy!

"I BELIEVE life is a spiritual journey, every struggle is a learning OPPORTUNITY for deeper SELF-EXPLORATION and PERSONAL GROWTH."

GRASS-FED BEEF

Balsamic Tenderloin with Garlic Basil Butter
Serves 6-8

A delightful way to-do dinner, this entree is amazing and good for all!

Ingredients
- 2.5-pound beef tenderloin roast
- kosher salt
- freshly ground black pepper
- 3 tablespoons grainy dijon mustard
- 1½ tablespoons aged balsamic vinegar
- 2 tablespoons *Garlic Basil Butter*, recipe page 142
- 3 cups spinach

Directions
Preheat oven to 500 degrees F. and line a baking sheet with tin foil.

Tie roast in 3-4 places with kitchen string/twine. Place roast on baking sheet, season generously with salt and pepper.

Mix mustard and balsamic vinegar in a small bowl and spread all over the top of the roast. Place roast in the oven for 35 minutes for a medium rare steak - medium steak.

Remove from oven, spread garlic basil butter on top, cover with tin foil and let rest for 10-15 minutes before slicing. Serve over a bed of spinach.

Garlic Basil Butter
Serves 4

This butter makes everything taste more delicious.

Ingredients
- ¾ cup finely chopped parsley
- 2 tablespoons finely chopped basil
- zest of 2 lemons
- 1 small garlic clove, minced
- 2 tablespoons of grass-fed butter

Directions
Combine all ingredients together in the food processor, mix until well combined.

"Without health, life is not life; it is only a state of languor and suffering." —Francois Rabelais, a major French Renaissance writer, doctor and humanist

GRILL-IT-UP

143

Pistachio Pesto Hanger Steak
Serves 4-6

This recipe brings gourmet to barbequing!

Ingredients
- 1 tablespoon MCT or coconut oil
- salt and pepper to taste
- ¼ cup extra virgin olive oil or more as needed
- 1-1 ½ pounds hanger steak
- 2 tablespoons *Pistachio Pesto Sauce*, recipe page 134
- 3 cups of spinach

Directions
Rub Steaks with MCT oil or coconut oil, set aside.

Heat grill pan or fire up the grill at medium-high heat. Season meat with sea salt, place on grill or in pan and reduce heat to medium-low. Cook 6-7 minutes per side for medium-rare.

Transfer steak to plate, top with pistachio pesto sauce and allow 5 minutes to rest. Slice the steak thinly across the grain and serve on a bed of spinach. Top with a squeeze of lemon. Enjoy!

Grilled Salmon with Kale Salad
Serves 2

A dinner loaded with healthy fat and protein to nourish your body.

Ingredients
- 2 tablespoons extra virgin olive oil
- 2 salmon fillets
- salt and pepper to taste
- 2 cups *Tuscan Kale Salad*, recipe page 96

Directions
Turn on grill to low medium heat and let warm up for 5 minutes. Rub both sides of salmon fillets in olive olive, season with salt and pepper.

Place salmon on grill and cook until flaky, 3 to 5 minutes on each side. Remove from grill and serve salmon over tuscan kale salad.

Grilled Shrimp with Satay Sauce
Serves 2-4

Everyone loves shrimp on the barbie served with bacon!!

Ingredients
- 1 ½-pounds fresh or frozen large shrimp in shells
- 3 tablespoons lemon juice
- black pepper to taste
- 1 large head of iceberg lettuce, cut into 12 wedges
- 2 slices bacon, cooked and crumbled
- ½ cup raw cashews, crushed
- 1 tablespoons coconut or MCT oil
- 2 tablespoons *Satay Sauce*, recipe opposite page

Directions
Thaw shrimp, if frozen. Peel and devein shrimp, leaving tails intact if desired. Rinse shrimp, pat dry with paper towels. In a medium bowl, combine shrimp, 2 tablespoons of lemon juice and teaspoon of black pepper, toss to coat. Set aside.

Thread shrimp onto six 10-12 inch skewers and rub with oil. Heat grill to low-to-medium heat. Place shrimp skewers on grill. Cook for 3 to 5 minutes or until shrimp are opaque, turning once halfway through.

Place shrimp on lettuce wedges drizzle with satay sauce and top with crushed cashews and bacon crumbles.

Satay Sauce
Serves 2-4

A super yummy and creamy sauce that's great on chicken, shrimp or veggies.

Ingredients
- ¾ cup almond butter
- ½ cup coconut milk
- 3 tablespoons braggs amino acids
- 2 tablespoons fresh grated ginger
- 2 tablespoons rice wine vinegar
- 1 tablespoon lime juice
- 2 teaspoons hot sauce

Directions
Whisk all ingredients together in bowl and serve.

Simply Grilled Fish+Cauliflower Couscous
Serves 4

This easy fish dinner is as equally healthy!

Ingredients
- 2 tablespoons fresh lemon juice, plus wedges for serving
- 1 tablespoon extra virgin olive oil
- 2 cloves garlic, chopped
- ¼ teaspoon salt and black pepper
- 4 tilapia fillets
- 1 cup *Cauliflower Couscous*, recipe page 155
- 1 tablespoon chopped fresh flat-leaf parsley

Directions
In a medium bowl, combine the lemon juice, oil, garlic, salt and pepper. Add the tilapia and toss to coat. Let marinate for 10 minutes.

Heat grill to high. Grill the tilapia until cooked through, 1 to 2 minutes per side. Serve over the couscous. Squeeze lemon wedges on top and sprinkle with parsley.

Spicy Garlic Mustard Chicken
Serves 2

If you love spicy foods this entree is perfect for you!

Ingredients
- 2 boneless skinless chicken breasts
- 1 tablespoon MCT or coconut oil
- 4 tablespoons grass-fed unsalted butter, at room temperature
- 1 tablespoon spicy brown mustard
- 1 teaspoon garlic powder
- 1 teaspoon hot sauce or sriracha
- 3 cups spinach
- pinch of sea salt

Directions
Rub 2 Chicken Breast with MCT oil or coconut oil and set aside.

In a small bowl combine: butter, hot sauce, garlic powder and spicy brown mustard, stirring well to combine.

Heat Grill pan or fire up the grill at medium-high heat. Season chicken breast with sea salt, place on grill or in pan and reduce heat to medium-low. Cook 8-10 minutes per side.

Transfer chicken to plate, top with hot sauce-mustard mixture and allow 5 minutes to rest. Slice into chicken strips and serve on a bed of spinach. Top with a drizzle of olive oil if desired.

Salmon Kebabs with Avocado Compound Butter
Serves 2-4

A fun and delicious way to-do kababs!

Ingredients
- 1-pound skinless salmon fillet, cut into 1 1/2-inch pieces
- salt and black pepper to taste
- ¼ cup olive oil
- 2 tablespoons *Avocado Compound Butter,* recipe opposite page
- 2 tablespoons chopped toasted pine nuts
- 2 teaspoons grated lemon zest

Directions
Heat grill to medium-high. Thread the salmon onto skewers, rub with oil, season with salt and pepper. Grill, turning occasionally, until opaque throughout, 4 to 6 minutes. Remove skewers from grill, spread cilantro butter on top of salmon and sprinkle with pine nuts. Serve.

*Great served with quinoa!

Avocado Compound Butter
Serves 2-4

A great way to use up those extra greens, adds zest to fish and chicken!

Ingredients
- 6 tablespoons grass-fed unsalted butter, at room temperature
- 6-ounces ripe avocado meat
- ½ cup cilantro, chopped
- 2 teaspoons cumin, ground
- 1 tablespoons fresh lime juice
- sea salt and ground pepper to taste
- ¼ teaspoon cayenne pepper (optional)

Directions
In the food processor combine all ingredients until well combined. Store in the fridge in an airtight container for 5 days.

SATISFYING SIDES

Bomb Curry Cauliflower "Rice"
Serves 6-8

This gluten-free cauliflower rice is a crowd pleaser you will love!

Ingredients
- 1 head of cauliflower
- 1 onion, chopped
- 2 cloves garlic, minced
- 1 sweet potato, cubed
- ½ cup roasted, salted peanuts
- 1 tablespoon mild curry powder
- 2 teaspoon smoked paprika
- 1 bunch fresh cilantro, chopped
- ¼ teaspoon stevia
- 2 teaspoon coconut or mct oil
- juice of 1 lime
- sea salt and pepper to taste
- hot sauce (optional)

Directions
To make cauliflower rice, break apart one head of cauliflower and place in a high powered blender or food processor. Process on medium until cauliflower takes on the consistency of rice— around two minutes. Set aside.

In a large skillet, saute sweet potato, onions and garlic in coconut oil for 10 minutes. Add spices, saute one more minute until fragrant. Add cauliflower, cook five minutes or until tender. Turn off heat and fold in stevia and peanuts and lime juice. Mix well.

Topped with cilantro, more peanuts and hot sauce if desired then serve!

Sesame Asparagus Spears
Serves 2-4

This chopped asparagus side dish tastes savory sweet.

Ingredients
- 3 tablespoons sesame oil
- 2 tablespoons white wine vinegar
- 2 tablespoons braggs amino acids
- ¼ teaspoon stevia
- sea salt
- 1-pound fairly thin pencil asparagus, ends trimmed, cut into 2-inch pieces
- 4 tablespoons sesame seeds

Directions
Bring a large pot of water to a rolling boil. In a medium bowl, whisk together the sesame oil, white wine vinegar, braggs, and stevia. Set aside.

Prepare an ice bath: Fill a large bowl halfway with ice cubes and add some cold water. Place a colander squarely inside the ice bath. The colander will keep you from having to pick the asparagus out from amongst the ice cubes in the ice bath.

Add salt until the boiling water tastes like seawater. Add the asparagus to the boiling water and cook for 1 1/2 to 2 minutes - you want them to be crunchy. If the asparagus are thin, cook for only 1 minute. Remove the asparagus from the water with a strainer and transfer them to the colander inside the ice bath. Allow them to cool completely for a few minutes and then place them on a kitchen towel to drain any excess moisture.

Heat a large skillet over high heat. Add the sesame mixture and green beans, toss a couple of times to coat everything evenly. Saute for a couple of minutes so the asparagus get caramelized. Transfer to a large platter and sprinkle with sesame seeds. Ready to serve.

Cauliflower Couscous
Serves 2-4

This is gluten-free recipe is a healthier alternative to rice and couscous.

Ingredients
- 1 small head cauliflower, cut into 1 inch florets
- 1 teaspoon extra virgin olive oil
- 2 tablespoons grass-fed unsalted butter
- 3 tablespoons water
- ½ lemon juiced
- 1 tablespoon rosemary, stems removed.
- ½ teaspoon garlic minced
- 1 tablespoon minced fresh chives
- ½ cup almonds, sliced
- sea salt and pepper

Directions
In food processor pulse the cauliflower and rosemary until finely chopped.

In large skillet combine the oil, butter, lemon, garlic and water heat over medium heat until butter melts. Add the cauliflower mixture and cook stirring often until tender, 6 to 8 mins.

Please couscous in a medium mixing bowl. Season with salt and pepper, add almonds. Toss to combine. Sprinkle with chives and serve!

Fire Sauteed Green Beans
Serves 2-4

A fiery side dish that is bold in flavor.

Ingredients
- 1 pound green beans
- 2 tablespoons sesame oil
- 3 teaspoons minced garlic
- 2 teaspoons grated or chopped fresh ginger
- ½ medium jalapeno, thinly sliced
- 2 tablespoons braggs amino acids
- ½ cup of sliced almonds

Directions
Wash green beans under cold running water. Cut off the root ends and discard. Bring a large pot of salted water to a boil over medium-high heat. Add the beans and blanch until bright green, about 2 minutes. Shock in ice water bath then drain in a colander.

Heat a large wok or skillet over high heat. Add the sesame oil, then add garlic, ginger and chile. Stir the mixture around so it fries in the oil and gets fragrant, about 30 seconds. Add the green beans and toss a couple of times to coat everything evenly.

Saute for a couple of minutes so the beans get a little caramelization. Add the braggs and almonds, cook for 1 to 2 more minutes; the beans should still be nice and crisp. Transfer to a large platter and serve.

Roasted Vegetables
Serves 4-6

A super healthy way to cook your vegetables.

Ingredients
- 2 red bell peppers, seeded and diced
- 1 cup white mushrooms
- 1 sweet potato, peeled and cubed
- 1 red onion, quartered
- 1 tablespoon fresh thyme, chopped
- 2 tablespoons fresh rosemary, chopped
- ¼ cup olive oil
- 2 tablespoons balsamic vinegar
- salt and freshly ground black pepper

Directions
Preheat oven to 475 degrees F.

In a large bowl, combine red bell peppers, sweet potato, and mushrooms. Separate the red onion quarters into pieces, and add them to the mixture.

In a small bowl, stir together thyme, rosemary, olive oil, vinegar, salt and pepper. Toss with vegetables until they are coated. Spread evenly on a large roasting pan.

Roast for 35 to 40 minutes in oven, stirring every 10 minutes or until vegetables are cooked through and browned.

Broccoli with Satay Sauce
Serves 2-4

A dish that powers your energy!

Ingredients
- 2 cups of steamed broccoli
- 3 tablespoons of *Satay Sauce*, recipe page 147
- ½ cup unsalted peanuts,
- 1 teaspoon chopped fresh parsley
- dash of crushed red pepper

Directions
Combine all ingredients together. Serve.

Candied Brussel Sprouts and Bacon
Serves 2-4

This side is like candy that you can't get enough of!

Ingredients
- 1 tablespoon of grass-fed unsalted butter
- 16-ounces chopped brussel sprouts
- ½ onion, chopped
- ½-pound chopped bacon
- sprinkle of stevia
- 1 tablespoon MCT or coconut oil
- sea salt and pepper to taste

Directions
In saute pan, heat coconut or MCT oil at medium heat. Add the bacon and onions then sprinkle stevia on top. Cook until brown then add the brussel sprouts and butter. Season with salt and pepper. Cook until bacon and brussel sprouts are crispy. Serve and enjoy!

Grilled Balsamic Vegetables
Serves 6-8

A sweet, tangy and healthy way to eat your veggies.

Ingredients
For Glaze
- 1 ½ cups balsamic vinegar, preferably aged
- ¼ teaspoon stevia
- 1 honeycrisp apple

For Veggies
- ½ cup balsamic vinegar, preferably aged
- ¼ cup extra-virgin olive oil
- 1 tablespoon sea salt
- 1 tablespoon freshly ground black pepper
- 1 teaspoon garlic powder
- 2 celery stalks, trimmed and cut in 1/4-inch slices
- 2 large red onions, cut into rounds, 3/8-inch thick
- 2 zucchinis, sliced lengthwise, 1/4-inch thick
- 2 cups, large white mushrooms,
- 2 tablespoons extra virgin olive oil

Directions
For the Balsamic glaze:
Combine vinegar, stevia, and apple in a food processor and puree. Add to a medium saute pan over medium heat, Let simmer for 15 to 20 minutes or until reduced by half. Keep warm for glazing on grill.

In a 1 gallon re-sealable bag, add the balsamic vinegar, olive oil, sea salt, pepper, and garlic and mix until combined. Next add celery root, zucchini, mushrooms and onions, remove excess air. Allow to marinate for 30 minutes. Remove from marinade and thread veggies on skewers.

Preheat grill to medium-high. Brush grill with oil. Cook veggies on both sides for 3 to 5 minutes brushing with balsamic glaze. Mark and brown evenly on both sides. Remove to pan, and cover until ready to serve.

Drizzle veggies with remaining glaze and serve on a warm platter.

Baked Asparagus Fries
Serves 2-4

A crunchy way to eat asparagus!

Ingredients
- 1 ½ cup almond meal
- 1 cup grated Parmesan cheese
- sea salt and black pepper to taste
- 1-pound asparagus, trimmed
- 2 large eggs, beaten

Directions
Preheat oven to 425 degrees F.

Lightly grease a baking sheet with grass-fed butter. In a large bowl, take almond meal and season with salt and pepper, to taste. Set aside.

Working in batches, dredge asparagus in flour, dip into eggs, then dredge in parmesan, pressing to coat. Place asparagus in a single layer onto the prepared baking sheet. Place into oven and bake for 10-12 minutes, or until golden brown and crisp. Serve immediately.

Coconut Whipped Cream+Fresh Berries
Serves 2-4

A healthy and unrefined dessert recipe for coconut lovers!

Ingredients
- 1 can full-fat coconut cream, refrigerated overnight
- ½ tablespoon vanilla extract
- ¼ teaspoon stevia
- dash of cardamon
- ½ cup fresh berries (strawberries, blueberries, raspberries)
- 2 squares of at least 70% cacao dark chocolate, chopped

Directions
Remove the cream from the fridge, carefully turn it upside down and open the can. Drain out as much of the liquid as possible from the top of the can and scoop out the solidified pure coconut cream.

Place the cream in a mixing bowl, whip the cream with a hand mixer for 4 minutes. Add the stevia, cardamon and vanilla powder, mix for 1 minute. Serve the coconut cream in small bowls and top with fresh berries and chopped dark chocolate.

Dessert Pecans
Serves 2-4

A sugar-free nutty dessert that you can feel good about.

Ingredients
- 2 cups almonds
- 1 egg white
- ½ teaspoon cinnamon
- ¼ teaspoon salt
- pinch of nutmeg
- ¼ teaspoon ginger powder

Directions
Preheat oven to 350 degrees fahrenheit.

Mix all dry ingredients together in a small mixing bowl. Then mix together almonds and egg whites in a medium mixing bowl. Mix together all spices and egg white almond mixture.

Grease cookie sheet and place almond mix onto pan. Cook for 20 minutes!

Oatmeal Chocolate Chunk Cookies
Serves 8-12

A gluten-free, refined sugar-free and protein packed super cookie that will leave you feeling light and energized!

Ingredients
- 1 cup grass-fed butter
- ¼ cup stevia
- 1 organic apple
- 3 organic eggs
- 1 ½ cup raw almond butter
- 3 cups gluten-free rolled oats
- ¾ cup almond meal
- ¾ cup vanilla whey protein powder
- 1 teaspoon MCT or coconut oil
- 1 teaspoon vanilla
- 2 teaspoons baking soda
- 1 teaspoon sea salt
- 2-ounces dark chocolate 70% cacao bar, chopped
- 2 cups of walnuts, chopped

Directions
Preheat oven to 350 degrees F.

In a medium saucepan melt butter, stevia and almond butter until smooth and creamy. Combine eggs, MCT oil and apple in a blender, mix until well blended.

Combine the almond meal, baking soda, salt, oats and protein powder in a large bowl. Stir into the creamed mixture. Mix in the chopped walnuts and dark chocolate until just combined. Drop by teaspoonfuls onto ungreased cookie sheets.

Bake for 10 to 15 minutes in the preheated oven, or until just light brown. Don't over-bake. Cool and store in an airtight container.

Vegan Cacao Hot Chocolate
Serves 1

This sweet recipe is delicious, unrefined and a craving crusher.

Ingredients
- 1 cup of almond milk
- 1 tablespoon of raw cacao
- teaspoon of cinnamon
- dash of stevia

Directions
Warm the milk, cacao and cinnamon on a low-medium heat. Add the stevia and serve.

Chocolate-Dipped Apples
Serves 4

This is a fun and healthy dessert option, great to-do with kids!

Ingredients
- 4 honeycrisp apples
- 8-ounces of at least 70% dark chocolate cacao
- ½ cup almonds, sliced
- 4 bamboo skewers

Directions
Wash and thoroughly dry the apples. Insert bamboo sticks into apple cores. Melt chocolate in double boilers. 1 at a time, gently dip the apples into the chocolate and roll around, making sure bottom half of apple is covered. Place on waxed paper. Dip the apple bottoms into a bowl of the sliced almonds.

Place dipped apples on waxed paper and refrigerate for 15 minutes to harden. Slice and serve.

Healthy Cookie Dough Protein Balls
Serves 12 balls

If you love cookie dough then you will love this sweet treat that's packed with protein!

Ingredients
- ¾ cup raw almond butter
- 1 tablespoon coconut flour, plus more if necessary
- ½ cup vanilla whey protein powder
- 1 teaspoon vanilla extract
- 1 tablespoon almond milk, plus more if necessary
- 2 tablespoons at least 70% cacao dark chocolate, chopped

Directions
In a large bowl, add all ingredients except chocolate. Mix together using a wooden spoon until ingredients are well combined and resemble a soft cookie dough. If it seems to dry add a teaspoon or two more almond milk. If too wet, add a teaspoon more of coconut flour. (The important note is that you'll want to be able to roll the dough into balls that stick together well.) Stir in dark chocolate chopped chunks, then roll into 12 tablespoon sized balls.

Ready to serve or transfer to an airtight container and store in fridge.

Chocolate Peanut Butter Balls
Serves 8 balls

Tastes like peanut butter cups but much healthier for you!

Ingredients
- ¾ cup gluten-free rolled oats
- ½ cup organic peanut butter
- ¼ teaspoon stevia
- 4-ounces at least 70% cacao dark chocolate

Directions
In a bowl combine oats, peanut butter and stevia. Stir well until combined. Score the mixture into quarters and form two balls out of each quarter (8 balls in total). Set balls on a cookie sheet lined with parchment paper until chocolate is ready.

In a small saucepan on low heat, melt dark chocolate stirring until smooth and completely melted. Using a spoon, gently roll ball around in the chocolate until well covered, using a fork gently allow excess chocolate to drip off and place ball back on the cookie sheet. Continue with remaining balls.

Place cookie sheet in the refrigerator until chocolate has hardened, about 15 minutes.

Once the chocolate has hardened, transfer the balls to a tupperware container and store them in the refrigerator or serve!

Healthy Fudgy Brownie Skillet
Serves 8

This dessert a chocolate lover's dreams without the guilt!

Ingredients
- 4 tablespoons coconut oil or MCT oil
- 1 cup dark chocolate at least 70% cacao, melted
- 2 tablespoons grass-fed butter, melted
- ¼ teaspoon salt
- 1 cup ripe avocado
- ½ cup cacao powder
- ¼ cup coconut palm sugar
- ½ teaspoon baking soda
- 2 teaspoon vanilla extract
- 2 eggs
- 2 tablespoons coconut milk
- ½ cup coconut flour
- ½ cup walnuts, chopped
- additional chopped dark chocolate for topping

Directions
Preheat oven to 350 degrees F.

Grease an 8 inch skillet. Place everything in a blender except the baking soda and puree until smooth. Pulse in baking soda and spread batter into prepared skillet.

Top with additional chocolate if desired and bake for 25-30 minutes until the edges start to pull away from the sides and the middle is still just slightly undercooked.

Remove from oven and let cool before serving. Enjoy!

Dark Chocolate Mousse
Serves 8

A delightful and healthy chocolate dessert, you won't believe how good it tastes!

Ingredients
Mousse
- 2 tablespoon almond milk
- 6 tablespoons grass-fed butter
- ½ teaspoon vanilla powder
- 6 large eggs
- ¼ teaspoons stevia
- 7-ounces dark chocolate at least 70% cacao
- ¼ teaspoon coarse sea salt
- 1 avocado, pitted and peeled.

Topping
- 1 cup coconut cream from a can of coconut milk, chilled
- 2 tablespoons coconut palm sugar
- 1 tablespoon cacao powder

Directions
In a heatproof bowl set over a sauce pan of barely simmer water (medium-low heat), heat butter, milk, vanilla powder, chocolate and salt stirring gently until melted 8 to 10 minutes. Transfer to blender, add avocado and puree until smooth. Using an electric mixer on medium-high speed, beat egg yolks and stevia in a medium bowl until pale and fluffy, about 5 minutes. Next, using electric mixer with clean beaters, beat egg whites about 3 minutes.

Using a large spatula, gently fold egg yolk mixture into chocolate mixture until no streaks remain. Starting in the center of the mixture and working your way toward the edges of the bowl, gently fold egg whites into chocolate mixture (make sure to scrape up from the bottom), rotating bowl as you go, until no streaks remain. Divide mousse among small bowls, smooth surface, and chill at least 4 hours. Mousse can be made 4 days ahead. Cover and keep chilled.

Topping - Whip cream and palm sugar together in a medium bowl until medium peaks form. Just before serving, spoon large dollops of whipped cream on top of each mousse and dust with cacao powder using a fine strainer.

German Chocolate Pecan Pie in a Coconut Crust
Serves 8

A gluten-free and low glycemic treat that won't spike your blood sugar and is great for the family!

Ingredients
Coconut Crust
- 3 1/3 cups dried, shredded coconut, divided
- 5 tablespoons coconut milk
- 2 tablespoons coconut or MCT oil

German Chocolate Pecan Pie Filling
- 4-ounces at least 70% cacao dark chocolate bar, chopped
- 2 eggs
- 5 tablespoons grass-fed butter
- ¼ teaspoon stevia
- ½ cup organic coconut palm sugar
- 1 cup dried, shredded coconut
- 7-ounce bag, raw sliced pecans

Directions
Coconut Crust - Preheat the oven to 350F. In a food processor, combine 2 cups dried shredded coconut, coconut milk, and coconut oil. Blend for 3-5 minutes or until the mixture turns sticky and holds together.

In a medium sized bowl, combine the coconut mixture plus an additional 1 1/3 cups dried coconut. Place the coconut mixture in a 10" pie dish. Gently, spread the coconut mixture so that it covers the pie dish. Press the coconut crust down into the pie dish so that it holds together well. Cover with a piece of parchment paper that's been cut with a large hole in the center to show the inner pie crust while covering the edge. Bake for 10-12 minutes.

German Chocolate Pecan Pie Filling - Preheat oven to 375F. Once the crust has been par-baked, remove parchment paper and add the chopped up chocolate bar to the bottom of the pie crust. In a medium sized bowl, whisk the 2 eggs together; set aside. In a heavy bottomed sauce pan, over medium-low heat, melt the butter. Add the stevia and coconut palm sugar, and then whisk it all together for 2-3 minutes; remove from heat and allow to cool for 5 minutes. Once cooled, slowly whisk the mixture into the eggs. Mix in the coconut and pecans. Pour the filling into the pie crust over the chocolate, and then bake for 22-25 minutes or until set.

NAKED CONFIDENCE LIFESTYLE RITUALS

Doggie Love

We love to spend quality time with our dog. Animals are angels that give you love.

Live Laugh Love

Nothing is more important to me than my husband. Make time and effort for those you love.

Josafat de la Toba

Travel

My parents live in Cabo. It's the best getaway to rest and recharge.

Yoga & Meditation

The key to staying stress-free mentally and physically

Soul Sisters

I surround myself with other women who lift me up!

Feed Your Mind

I'm always reading a book that expands my mind.

Build Your Strength

I love to sweat with high intensity interval training using light weights or my body weight at least 3 times every week.

NOW you have all the **KNOWLEDGE** and tools you need to be your **HIGHEST WELL-BEING & SELF**. The key to sustainable **HEALTH** is to **STAY MOTIVATED & IMPLEMENT** everything you have learned into your **DAILY LIFE**. There is no turning back only **FLYING HIGHER**. You can start to develop **DAILY RITUALS** to keep your **MIND & BODY STRONG**. Live **HAPPY & SHINE BRIGHT!**

Xo, Cort

References and Resources

Here are my resources for your edification and knowledge, organized by each section in The Naked Confidence Cookbook. Feel free to visit my website cortneycribari.com for more of my favorite books, kitchen and eating tips, stories and many more recommendations and resources.

Honor Your Body - Realizing There's A Problem
These experts, organizations and published journals specialize in the fields of psychology and eating disorders.
- https://www.nationaleatingdisorders.org/get-facts-eating-disorders
- https://www.google.com/webhp?sourceid=chrome-instant&ion=1&espv=2&ie=UTF-8#q=def%20of%20eating%20disorder
- Wade, T. D., Keski-Rahkonen A., & Hudson J. (2011).Epidemiology of eating disorders. In M. Tsuang and M. Tohen (Eds.), Textbook inPsychiatric Epidemiology (3rd ed.) (pp. 343-360). New York: Wiley.
- Smolak, L. (2011). Body image development in childhood. In T. Cash & L. Smolak (Eds.)

Be Honest With Yourself - Facing A Problem
- http://www.eatingdisorderhope.com/information/statistics-studies#Binge-Eating-Disorder-Statistics
- Neumark Sztainer, D. (2005). I'm, Like, SO Fat! New York: The Guilford Press. pp. 5.
- Body Image: A Handbook of Science, Practice, and Prevention (2nd ed.).New York: Guilford.

Protect Yourself - Leaving a Toxic Relationship
These experts, organizations and published journals specialize in the fields of mental health and drug use.
- [1]: Substance Abuse and Mental Health Services Administration. Results from the 2007 National Survey on Drug Use and Health: National findings (DHHS Publication No. SMA 08-4343) Rockville, MD: Office of Applied Studies; 2008.
- [2]: Johnston LD, O'Malley PM, Bachman JG, Schulenberg JE. Monitoring the Future national survey results on drug use, 1975–2006: Volume II, College students and adults ages 19–45 (NIH Publication No. 07-6206) Bethesda, MD: National Institute on Drug Abuse; 2007
- Kasperski, Sarah, et al. College students' use of cocaine: results from a longitudinal study. Addict Behav Apr 2011; 36(4): 408-411.

Get Educated About What You Eat - Stopping Diet Pills
- http://lighthouserecoveryinstitute.com/diet-pill-addiction-facts/

Choose Health Over Money - Managing a Stressful Job
- http://www.apa.org/monitor/2011/01/stressed-america.aspx

Love Yourself More - Dealing with Divorce
- http://www.divorcestatistics.org/

Losing Weight With Ease - Mastering The Process
These experts, organizations and articles specialize in the fields of health, obesity and disease.
- http://spokeonline.com/2015/02/war-continues-on-sugar-and-obesity
- http://www.nydailynews.com/life-style/health/researcher-sugar-addictive-cocaine-obesity-diabetes-cancer-heart-disease-article-1.1054419
- http://www.dailymail.co.uk/news/article-146021/Most-women-unhappy-bodies.html
- http://www.thyroid.org/media-main/about-hypothyroidism/
- http://www.cavemandoctor.com/2012/03/27/inflammation-which-foods-take-the-blame
- National Institute of Diabetes & Digestive & Kidney Diseases

Love What You See In The Mirror - Overcoming Body Shaming
- https://www.insighthealthcare.org/our-services/talking-therapies/nottingham/types-of-difficulties/low-self-esteem/

Cooking Preparation Steps
- http://www.prevention.com/food/healthy-eating-tips/top-reasons-choose-organic-foods
- http://www.ciwf.org.uk/your-food/eggs/
- http://well.blogs.nytimes.com/2010/03/11/switching-to-grass-fed-beef/?_r=0
- http://download.springer.com/static/pdf/690/art%253A10.1186%252F1475-2891-9-10.pdf?originUrl=http%3A%2F%2Fnutritionj.biomedcentral.com%2Farticle%2F10.1186%2F1475-2891-9-10&token2=exp=1459398877~acl=%2Fstatic%2Fpdf%2F690%2Fart%25253A10.1186%25252F1475-2891-9-10.pdf*~hmac=311084050bd9afe-6b72e0051cf0f314d73ea867c4ab3893cfa7527bf3819f126

Index

autoimmune issues, 22, 25, 36-37
    IBS, 25
    Hashimoto's Thyroiditis, 36-37
balance, 35
body shaming, 40-41
breakfast recipes, 61
    Almond Energy Pancakes, 74
    Fancy Oatmeal, 76
    Gluten-Free Apple Cinnamon Pancakes, 72
    Homemade Chicken + Apple Sausage, 70
    Lobster + Asparagus Frittata, 69
    Mushroom + Artichoke Scramble, 64
    OMG Scramble, 65
    Overnight Oats, 71
    Protein Scramble, 66
    Salmon Benedict, 67
    Super Coffee, 61
    Tomato Feta Scramble, 62
candida overgrowth, 37
cellulite, 40
challenge, 29, 40
cleansing, 36-38
confidence, 32-33, 41, 44-45
depression, 27, 44-46
dessert recipes, 161
    Chocolate Peanut Butter Balls, 167
    Coconut Whipped Cream+Fresh Berries, 162
    Dark Chocolate Mousse, 170
    Dessert Pecans, 163
    German Chocolate Pecan Pie in a Coconut Crust, 171
    Healthy Cookie Dough Protein Balls, 166
    Healthy Fudgy Brownie Skillet, 169
    Oatmeal Chocolate Chunk Cookies, 164
    Vegan Cacao Hot Chocolate, 165
diet pills, 22-23, 44
digestive issues, 27-28, 32
dinner recipes, 127
    Almond Crusted Salmon With Sauted Spinach, 138
    Baked Chicken Breast with Mushrooms & Spinach, 128
    Balsamic Tenderloin with Garlic Basil Butter, 141
    Brussel Sprouts+Bacon+Cauliflower Casserole, 127
    Grilled Salmon with Kale Salad, 145
    Grilled Shrimp with Satay Sauce, 146
    Healthier Than Mom's Meatloaf, 133
    Healthy Baked 'Fried' Chicken, 130
    Jerk Chicken with Avocado Compound Butter, 129
    Macadamia & Parmesan Crusted Tilapia, 137
    Quinoa Stir-fry with Chicken & Veggies, 131
    Parmesan Crusted Chicken, 132
    Pistachio Pesto Hanger Steak, 144
    Salmon Kebabs with Avocado Compound Butter, 150
    Salmon with Lemon, Asparagus and Rosemary, 139
    Simply Grilled Fish+Cauliflower Couscous, 148
    Spicy Garlic Mustard Chicken, 149
    Turkey Pesto Meatballs, 135
dressing, sauce & side recipes
    Avocado Compound Butter, 151
    Baked Asparagus Fries, 160
    Balsamic Vinaigrette Dressing, 108
    Bomb Curry Cauliflower "Rice", 153
    Broccoli with Satay Sauce, 158
    Candied Brussel Sprouts and Bacon, 158
    Champagne Vinaigrette Dressing, 109
    Cauliflower Couscous, 155
    Dijon Mustard Dressing, 106
    Fire Sauteed Green Beans, 156
    Garlic Basil Butter, 142
    Grilled Balsamic Vegetables, 159
    Healthy Tarter Sauce, 128
    Pistachio Pesto Sauce, 134
    Roasted Vegetables, 157
    Sesame Asparagus Spears, 154
    Sesame Dressing, 102
    Satay Sauce, 147
drinking, 27-29, 52
drugs, 17-19, 44
eating disorders, 14-16, 22, 27-29, 36, 44
food addiction, 38, 44
food shaming, 34-35
free-range foods, 47-48
gluten, 36-38, 40-41, 44, 52
grass-fed foods, 47-48, 50
healthy fats, 39, 48, 55-56
inflammation, 37-38
intermittent fasting, 36, 56
lunch recipes, 95
    Arugula Salad, 107
    Broccoli Feta Salad, 109
    Bunless Bacon & Avocado Burgers, 115
    Bunless Salmon Burgers, 117

    Butternut Squash Soup, 112
    Chicken Avocado Salad, 105
    Chopped Chicken Lettuce Wraps, 108
    Dream of Broccoli Soup, 111
    Grilled Romaine Salad, 110
    Grilled Salmon Arugula Salad, 98
    Grilled Vegetable Salad, 106
    Ground Turkey BLT Salad, 95
    Healthy Shredded Chicken Taco Salad, 104
    Lettuce Wrapped Bison Burgers, 116
    Raw Zucchini Noodle Salad, 101
    Simple Shredded Chicken, 103
    Spicy Shrimp Salad, 99
    Superwoman Salad, 107
    Thai Chicken Salad, 102
    Turkey, Kale & Brown Rice Soup, 113
    Tuscan Kale Salad, 96
    Zucchini Noodles, 100
mantras, 15, 16, 19, 22, 26, 28, 29, 33, 35, 38, 41, 44
organic foods, 47, 50, 55
purpose, 32, 57
relationships, 20-22, 25, 27-29, 32-33
    dating, 28-29
    divorce, 27
    toxic relationships, 17-19, 44
shakes & smoothie recipes, 79
    Antioxidant Refresher, 81
    Apple Almond Smoothie, 88
    Berry Bliss Protein Shake, 90
    Blueberry Chocolate Antioxidant Shake, 90
    Chocolate Supreme Protein Shake, 86
    Cinnamon Berry Shake, 91
    Ginger Coconut Shake, 88
    Green Goddess, 82
    Mocha Freeze, 93
    Peanut Butter Chocolate Protein Shake, 93
    Spiced Frappuccino Protein Shake, 87
    The Good Start, 79
slow-acting carbs, 39, 48, 50, 55-56
snack recipes, 119
    Kale & Artichoke Dip with Cucumber, 119
    Kale Chips, 123
    Nut Mix, 123
    Oatmeal Fiber Bars, 121
    Peanut Butter Sushi Bites, 125
    Sauteed Almonds, 124
    Spicy Cauliflower Bites, 122
sugar, 36-38, 40-41, 44, 52, 57
stress, 25-26
willpower, 23-24, 44

ABOUT THE AUTHOR

Since experiencing a series of health and eating struggles that began at the age of 16, Cortney Cribari has committed herself to regaining personal health, happiness and confidence. After taking years to heal her body; after spending thousands of dollars working with western medicine MDs, nutritionists, naturopathic doctors and practitioners; and after becoming a certified yoga and fitness instructor, as well as an expert on healthy living, Cortney is now on the other side.

She is a former corporate banking consultant turned health entrepreneur. In 2012, Cortney Cribari created a healthy living blog, called beautybreakthru.com, to help women who shared her struggles. Using her unique combination of passion, personal story, practical experience and professional expertise, she inspires and motivates others to live happier and healthier lives.

Cortney has a deep passion for health and fitness. From doing a fitness commercial shoot for a national brand in Los Angeles, to teaching people how to burn fat and find their zen in her yoga sculpt class, to private celebrity training and workouts; she is known to many as their personal weight loss coach online.

In her first book, The Naked Confidence Cookbook, Cortney offers a guided tour to your highest well-being one recipe at a time.

She lives with her husband and French bulldog in Los Angeles. Visit her at cortneycribari.com and connect with her on social media @cortneycribari on Instagram and Facebook.